THE BULLSEYE SITE, 11-Ge-127: A FLOODPLAIN ARCHAIC MORTUARY SITE IN THE LOWER ILLINOIS RIVER VALLEY.

PART ONE: PRELIMINARY SUMMARY AND INTERPRETATION OF THE 1984 INVESTIGATION AT THE BULLSEYE SITE, 11-Ge-127.

by
Harold Hassen
Illinois State Museum

PART TWO: PRELIMINARY EVALUATION OF BANNERSTONES AND OTHER GROUND-STONE ARTIFACTS IN THE WEAR COLLECTION FROM THE BULLSEYE SITE, 11-Ge-127.

by
Kenneth B. Farnsworth
Kampsville Archeological Center
Center for American Archeology

ILLINOIS STATE MUSEUM
Reports of Investigations, No. 42

Illinois State Museum
Springfield, Illinois
1987

Printed by Authority of the State of Illinois

1987
ISSN 0360-0270
ISBN 0-897792-110-0
Printed by Authority
of the State of
Illinois

CONTENTS

PART ONE: PRELIMINARY SUMMARY AND INTERPRETATIONS OF THE 1984 INVESTIGATIONS AT THE BULLSEYE SITE, 11-Ge-127

PART TWO: PRELIMINARY EVALUATION OF BANNERSTONES AND OTHER GROUND-STONE ARTIFACTS IN THE WEAR COLLECTION FROM THE BULLSEYE SITE, 11-Ge-127

FIGURES

TABLE

ACKNOWLEDGEMENTS

We thank the Robert Wear family, and especially Jim Wear, for bringing their Bullseye site excavations and artifacts to our attention and for making the material available for us to study. We are grateful to Michael D. Wiant who provided many constructive comments on earlier drafts of this paper. Marjorie B. Schroeder made the illustrations and provided editorial assistance. Excavations at the Bullseye site would not have been possible without the financial support of the Army Corps of Engineers, St. Louis District, and the Center for American Archeology. Lyle W. Konigsberg and Karen Atwell provided valuable field identifications of human bone. The artifact photographs were provided by Kenneth B. Farnsworth. Edwin Hajic allowed access to the aerial photographs. Additional photographic assistance was provided by Marlin Roos. The review comments provided by James Stoltman, Jane Buikstra, and Bonnie Styles are most appreciated. Nancy Wells assisted with technical editing. Timothy Osburn created and executed the page layouts. The cover was designed by Julianne Snider.

PART ONE: PRELIMINARY SUMMARY AND INTERPRETATIONS OF THE 1984 INVESTIGATIONS AT THE BULLSEYE SITE, 11-Ge-127

by

Harold Hassen

INTRODUCTION

Beginning in 1980 the Army Corps of Engineers, St. Louis District, initiated a series of contracts with the Center for American Archeology (CAA) to conduct surveys of lower Illinois River valley cultural resources (Hassen 1985b; Hassen and Batura 1983; Hassen and Hajic 1984), site evaluation studies (Batura and Leigh 1983, Hassen 1985a), and lower Illinois River Holocene floodplain geomorphological studies (Hajic 1981a, b, 1983; Hajic and Hassen 1980; Hajic and Leigh 1985). These projects were initiated as part of a comprehensive flood control study by the Army Corps of Engineers, St. Louis District.

This report presents summary information on the Bullseye site, 11-Ge-127, based on both the 1983 amateur excavations and the professional archaeological site evaluation study conducted in 1984 by the CAA (Hassen 1985a). Investigations at the site are continuing in cooperation with Dr. Jane Buikstra and the University of Chicago field school. It is expected that once excavations at the site are completed a more compre-hensive analytical study will be published. However, because of the exceptional nature of the site this preliminary report is warranted.

The Bullseye site, is located in Greene County, Illinois, on the eastern floodplain of the Illinois River. As of 1984 the site had produced a remarkable artifact assemblage. Included among the artifacts are: 29 bannerstones, 296 stemmed bifaces, 43 ground-stone axes, 1 drilled plummet, 1 tubular pipe, 4 copper awls and 45 drills. Some of these artifacts were found in human graves. When reference is made to stemmed bifaces, the term stem is used to denote that portion of the artifact designed for hafting and thus may include notched and unnotched varieties.

The site first came to the attention of professional archaeologists during an archaeological survey conducted in 1981 by the CAA for the Army Corps of Engineers (Hassen and Batura 1983). Prior to this survey the site was known to the landowner; through the years the Wear family had collected artifacts from the surface.

PROJECT AREA

The Bullseye site is located along the eastern margin of the Keach School Terrace approximately 2 km west of the Illinois River valley bluffs (Figures 1-3). The Keach School Terrace is a T1 terrace exposed since approximately 9950 B.P. (Hajic 1983). The Keach School Terrace was first defined by Butzer (1977) based on a type section located approximately 12 km south of the Bullseye site. Butzer (1977:19) described the upper 1.2 m as a massive zone of coarse sandy silt that probably was not deposited by the more recent low-energy flood silts. Evidence for the coarse nature of these deposits was re-

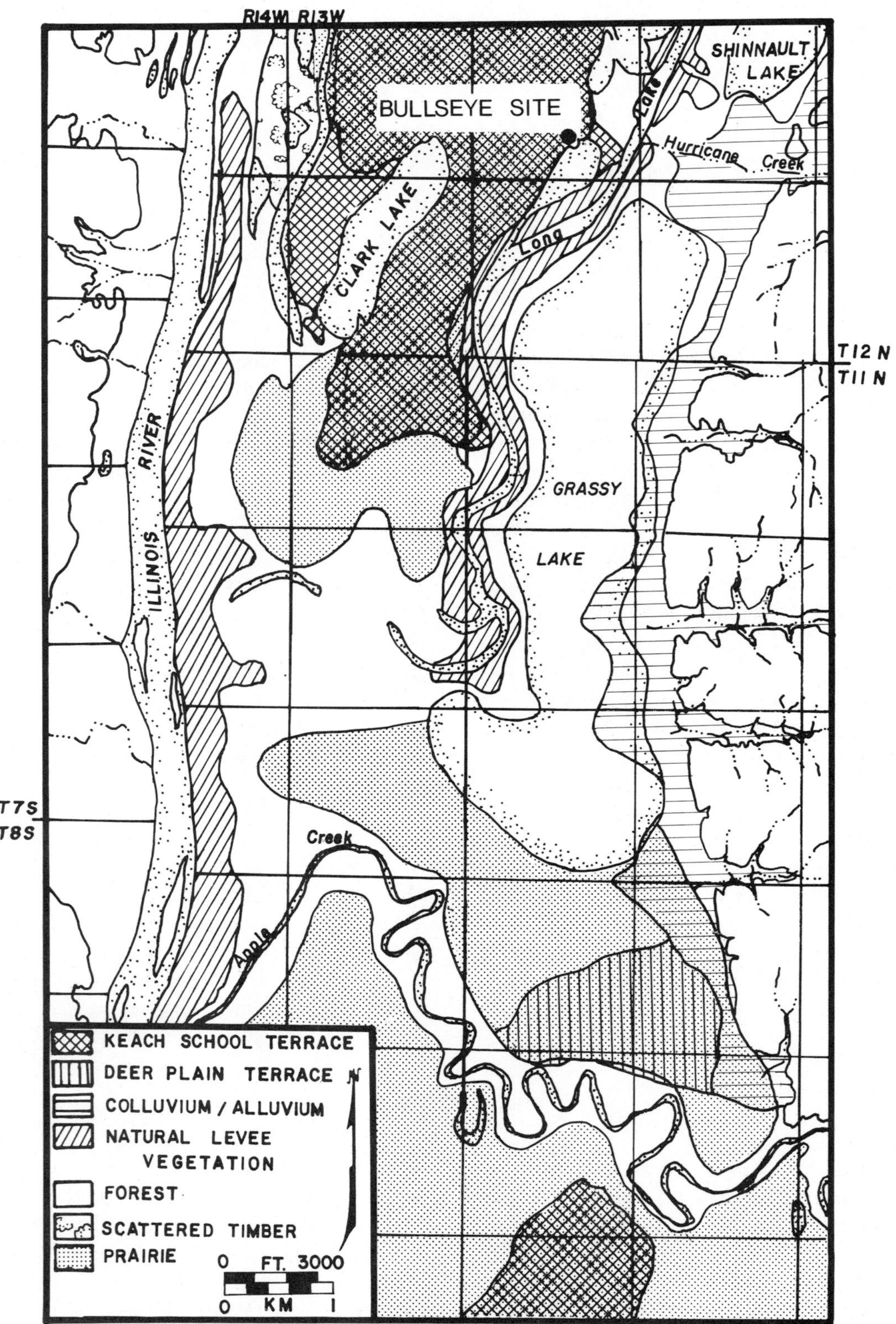

Figure 1. Early nineteenth-century vegetation of the Hartwell Drainage and Levee District and the location of the Bullseye site (after Asch and Asch, in Hassen and Batura 1983).

Figure 2. Aerial view of the Bullseye site and vicinity. (Photograph courtesy of Edwin Hajic and David Leigh.)

corded at the Bullseye site by the presence of large quantities of pebbles throughout the excavations. Along the eastern portion of the terrace, where the site is located, stream meandering within the Swan Lake paleo-channel has produced an irregularly serrated edge (Hajic 1983). Hay Pen Lake and Long Lake were located south and east of the site. These lakes are now drained. Abandoned channels to the south, west, and east appear to represent abandoned Hurricane Creek channels. The site elevation is between 129.75 and 130.4 m ASL. The soil is Bloomfield fine sand. It is unclear whether the sandy soil might also represent dunes above the Keach School Terrace surface. This is a well-drained, slightly acidic soil developed in wind- and water-deposited sand under a mixed hardwood forest (Downey et al. 1974). However, most of the prenineteenth-century vegetation of the Keach School Terrace was probably prairie (Asch and Asch 1982).

Figure 3. Close-up aerial view of the Bullseye site. (Photograph courtesy of Edwin Hajic and David Leigh.)

PREVIOUS INVESTIGATIONS

During the 1981 CAA survey, one Early Archaic Beaver Lake Lanceolate biface, four Middle Archaic side-notched stemmed bifaces, and a large quantity of Early Woodland Black Sand ceramics were recovered. The only recognized concentrations consisted of human and nonhuman bone and igneous cobbles.

After a prolonged flood in 1983 the field containing the Bullseye site was deeply plowed (approximately 30 cm) for the first time. During the plowing a bannerstone was observed on the surface. Bannerstones had not been previously found at the site. In addition, the density of surface artifacts was observed to be much greater when compared to the surface density prior to the 1983 plowing (Jim Wear, personal communication, 1984). Based on the identification of human burials and the recovery of predominantly side-notched stemmed bifaces during limited hand excavations conducted by the landowner and amateur archaeologists in the fall 1983, it became clear that an important Archaic site was represented. In the spring of 1984, permission was granted by the Wear family for CAA archaeologists to conduct investigations at the site. The investigations were directed by the author and the work was funded by the Army Corps of Engineers and the Center for American Archeology. Due to the types of artifacts exposed and recovered by the landowner, the focus of fieldwork at the Bullseye site shifted from the Early Woodland materials to the Archaic deposits. Previously, no large Archaic floodplain mortuary sites had been intensively analyzed from the lower Illinois River valley. A site similar to Bullseye is the Godar site, situated on a floodplain terrace on the western side of the Illinois River directly across from the Koster site. When this site was excavated in 1940, it produced 400 stemmed bifaces, 24 bannerstones, 25 grooved axes, and other assorted lithic artifacts (Titterington 1950). However, these collections are dispersed, and the site has never been fully analyzed.

FIELD STRATEGY

Prior to the investigations conducted by the CAA, local amateur archaeologists excavated an area approximately 20 x 15 m (Figure 4). These excavations were restricted to an area of dense lithic material corresponding to the surface location of the bannerstone and many diagnostic Archaic stemmed bifaces. The amateur excavations proceeded in an irregular fashion, exposing vertical rather than horizontal profiles. The vertical and horizontal dimensions of these excavations were expanded until the artifact densities were greatly diminished. A sifting box with 2.6-cm hardware mesh was used to screen sediments. The screening of sediments, however, was not continued on a routine basis. Although field notes were not kept, some artifacts were photographed as they were exposed; a sketch map was prepared illustrating bannerstone locations.

The area of the site excavated by the amateurs was limited but yielded an amazingly high number of bannerstones, axes, stemmed bifaces, and drills. Although artifacts were found below the plowzone and occasionally next to human bone, the sandy matrix contributed to poor bone preservation and also made it difficult to distinguish pit outlines. Consequently, despite the excavations by the amateurs, important contextual questions remained unanswered.

The goals of the CAA investigations were threefold:

1) to establish the vertical and horizontal distribution of artifacts and human burials across the entire site;
2) to recover, in situ, chronologically diagnostic artifacts;
3) to assess the degree of preservation and contextual integrity of the cultural remains.

To accomplish these tasks a series of nine 2 x 2 m units were excavated (Figure 5). Arbitrary excavation levels of 5 cm were used below the plowzone. All sediment including

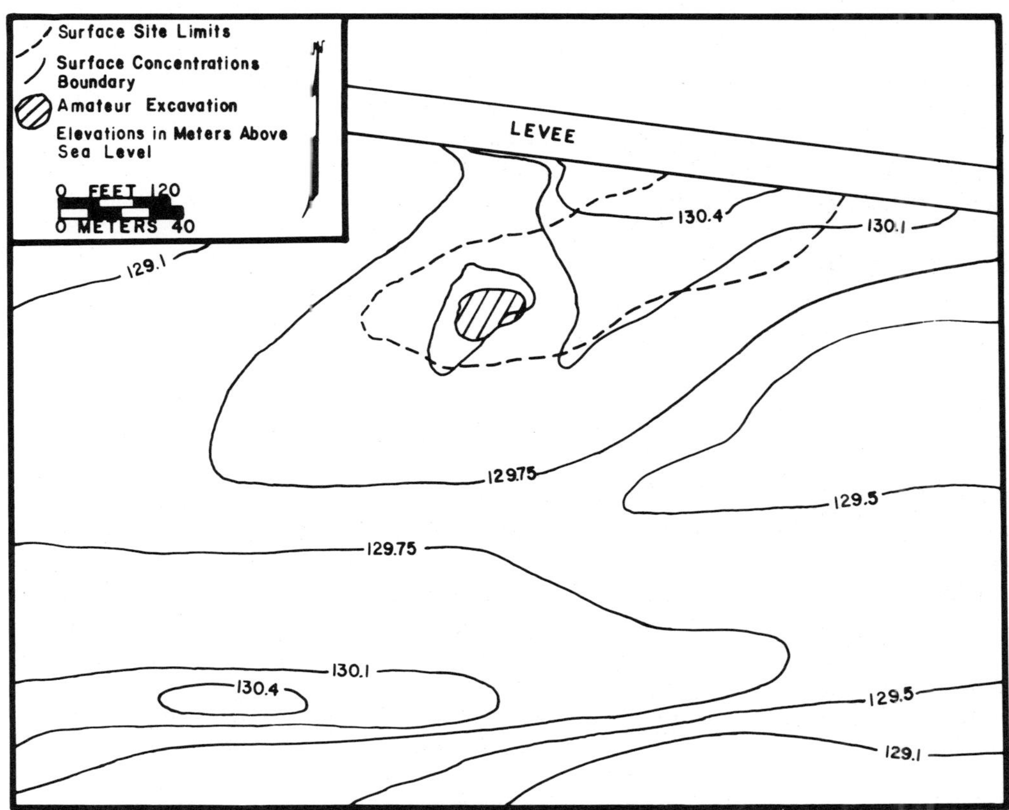

Figure 4. Topography and surface patterns, Bullseye site.

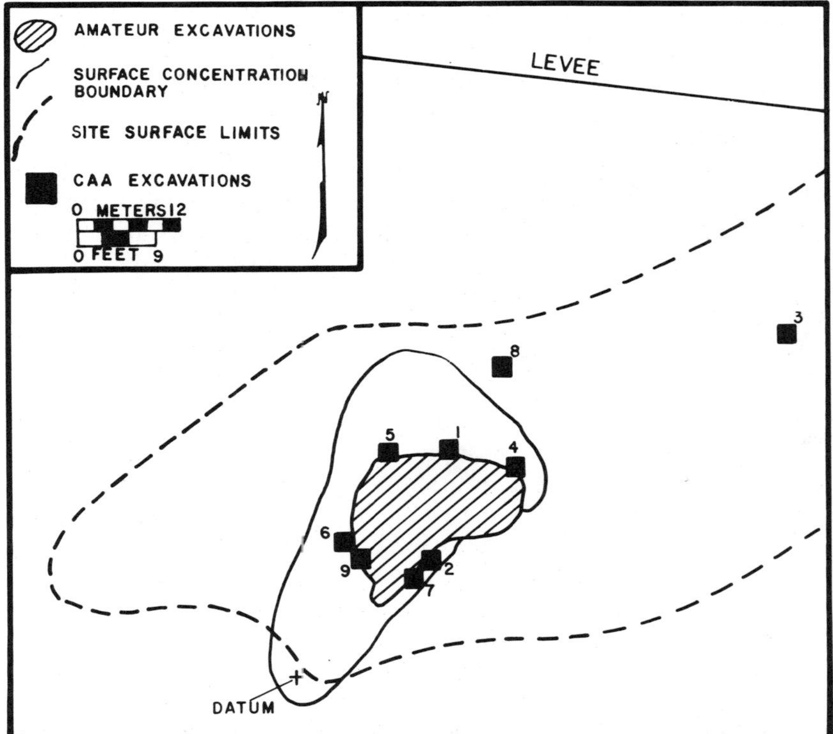

Figure 5. Excavation units at the Bullseye site.

the plowzone was screened through 0.6-cm hardware mesh. Flotation samples, approximately 12-15 l of sediment each, were recovered from each excavation level. Seven units were established along the margins of the amateur excavations because substantial quantities of bannerstones and stemmed bifaces were recovered in these areas, and profile walls indicated the presence of human burials in or near the units. Two units were situated between the artificial levee bordering Hurricane Creek and the amateur excavations.

RESULTS

Summary of Excavations

Based on interviews with the amateurs, examination of exposed profiles and debris densities, most of the human bone and diagnostic artifacts seemed to be contained within a zone 10-30 cm below the base of the well-defined plowzone (Figure 6) (40-60 cm below ground surface [b.g.s.]). Preliminary examination of frequency polygons for flakes and blocky fragments indicated a similar distribution. Although the sandy matrix resulted in the spatial displacement of some artifacts, in situ artifacts were found below the plowzone. Unfortunately, it was not possible to identify sediment differences attributable to pit features. Since extensive deposition onto the Keach School Terrace surface was unlikely, it was assumed that many of the artifacts found 10-30 cm below the plowzone were originally contained in pit features of varying depths. However, due to leaching in the sandy matrix, the boundaries of the pits were masked. It is also probable that the sandy matrix enhanced vertical artifact displacement.

The profile developed for the eastern wall of unit 1 was representative for the site (Figure 7). Bone preservation at the site was poor, but in some instances careful excavation permitted element identification and determination of burial orientation and position. The number of human burials exposed during the amateur excavations is unknown but estimated to be at least ten (Jim Wear, personal communication). Four of the CAA excavation units contained human burials below the plowzone (Figure 8). Two of the four human burials identified during the CAA excavations were flexed. A determination of the position of the other two individuals was not possible. One of the graves contained two individuals. One of the flexed burials was tentatively identified as a young adult.

Unit 1 contained two burials, Burial 4 and 5. Burial 5 was identified directly below the plowzone (30 cm b.g.s.), and it was assumed that portions were incorporated into the plowzone. The cranium and long bone fragments extended 45-50 cm b.g.s. All the bones were contained in a 20- to 25-cm-thick zone. Burial 4 was discovered 20 cm beneath

Figure 6. Amateur excavations, north wall profile with plowzone, Bullseye site.

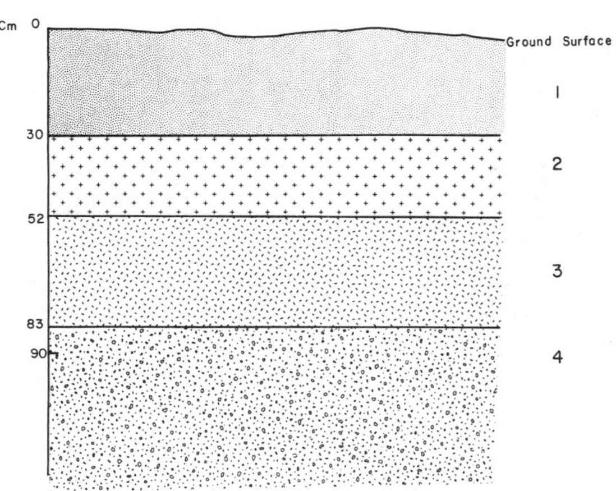

Figure 7. Unit 1, east wall profile, Bullseye site.
Stratum 1. plowzone, 0-30 cm below ground surface
(b.g.s), loamy fine sand, 10YR3/3 to 4/3.
Stratum 2. 31-52 cm b.g.s., fine sandy loam, 10YR4/3,
iron manganese concretions, very firm, coarse
subangular blocky structure.
Stratum 3. 53-83 cm b.g.s., fine sandy loam, 10YR4/4,
coarse very firm, subangular blocky structure, some
mottling, 10YR4/6 and 10YR5/4.
Stratum 4. 84-90 cm b.g.s. fine sand, 10YR4/4 to 5/4,
loose, coarse subangular blocky structure, some
mottling 10YR4/4.

A single chert core was found lying on top of the cranium. In addition to Burial 1, unit 2 also contained several disarticulated bone fragments. Several bones, consisting of pieces from a long bone and a mandible fragment with teeth, were recovered in the NE quarter directly beneath the plowzone. It is unknown whether a single individual was represented. All the bones were contained in a 5- to 10-cm-thick zone. Whether these bones occurred in the pit that probably contained Burial 1 is unknown. A second concentration of disarticulated bones was found in the SW quarter 120 cm from Burial 1 and approximately 30-35 cm b.g.s. Given their distance from Burial 1 it is possible that a second burial pit may have been present.

Unit 8 contained Burial 2. This concentration of several long bones was identified 35-45 cm b.g.s. The orientation of the long bones suggested that the burial may have been flexed and oriented north/south. The small size of the long bones indicated the individual was a juvenile. Unit 5 contained Burial 3, which consisted of skull fragments and long bones directly below the plowzone (35-40 cm b.g.s.). This burial was only partially exposed before the excavations were concluded in 1984. Given the distribution of

Burial 5 and was approximately 70 cm b.g.s. Despite extremely poor preservation, several rib fragments and teeth were recovered. All bones were contained in a 6- to 7-cm-thick zone.

Unit 2 contained Burial 1 (Figure 9). The burial was identified in the SW quarter 45 cm b.g.s. and was restricted to a 7-cm-thick zone. This flexed burial was oriented with the cranium to the southwest and the femur and tibia to the northeast.

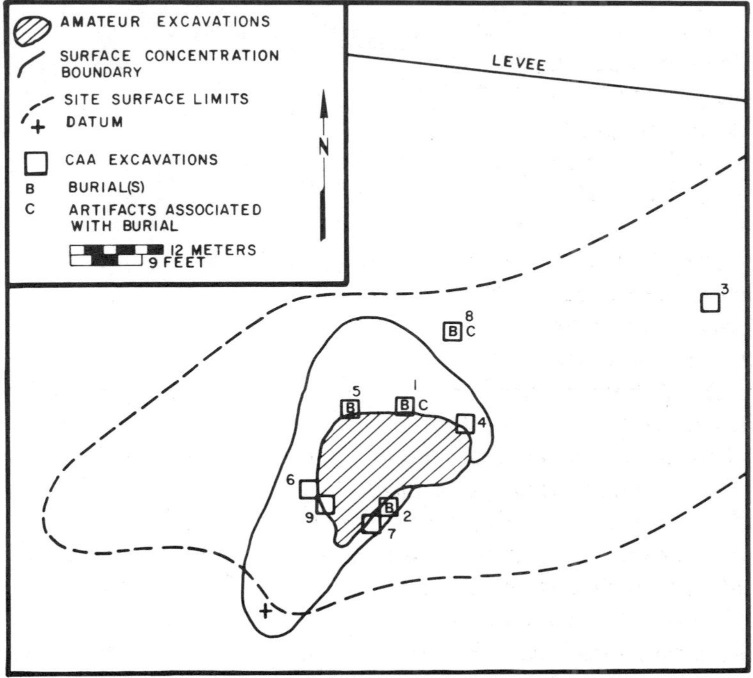

Figure 8. Burial locations, CAA excavations, Bullseye site.

human teeth and bone across the site surface, in profile walls, and within the backdirt pile resulting from the excavations by the amateurs, it is clear that additional human burials are present.

Despite disturbances due to both cultural and natural processes, excavations in 1984 by the CAA demonstrated the presence of temporally diagnostic artifacts with human burials. In Burial 4 of unit 1, a side-notched stemmed biface with a shallow concave base was lying atop a human rib fragment approximately 70 cm b.g.s. (Figure 10). The morphology of this artifact is similar to other stemmed bifaces found at the Quasar (Hassen 1985a), Napoleon Hollow (Michael D. Wiant, personal communication 1985), and Koster Middle Archaic deposits (Brown and Vierra 1983) postdating 6300 B.P.

In excavation unit 8 an artifact cache was recovered 10 cm below the base of the plowzone

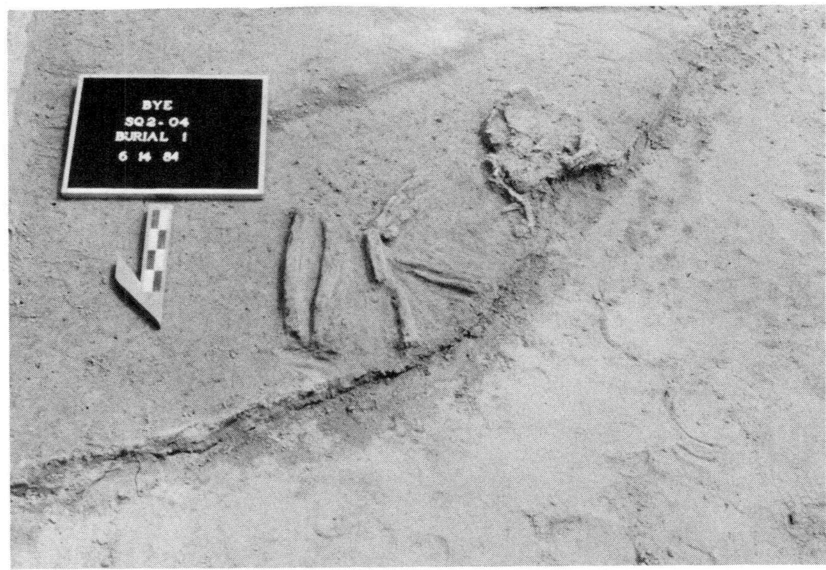

Figure 9. Unit 2, Burial 1, Bullseye site.

Figure 10. Middle Archaic side-notched stemmed biface, unit 1, Burial 4, Bullseye site.

(Figure 11). A human burial (no. 2) was located 50 cm to the southwest at an equal depth. This artifact cache consisted of three shallow side-notched stemmed bifaces, two unstemmed bifaces, a drill, and galena. From the same excavation level three additional side-notched stemmed bifaces were recovered during the screening of sediments.

So far, excavations have failed to produce any charcoal. The absence of charcoal is probably related to the sandy matrix.

Artifact analysis is continuing, but some preliminary counts and observations are offered. The diversity of lithic artifacts suggests a range of technological and functional categories. Artifact categories include bannerstones, stemmed bifaces, drills, axes, copper awls, a plummet, a pipe, hammerstones, manos, and assorted bifacial and unifacial items. Large quantities of

Figure 11. Artifact cache, unit 8, Burial 2.

ceramics are primarily restricted to the extreme eastern portion of the site. Given the ubiquitous presence of nondiagnostic lithic artifacts across the site surface and below the plowzone, it is unlikely that they would be restricted to the Early Woodland component. Whether these artifacts are restricted to activities exclusively confined to an Archaic mortuary context is uncertain.

manufacturing debris, flakes, and blocky fragments were also recovered. The relative absence of cortex on the manufacturing debitage suggests that either primary reduction involving cortex-covered pieces occurred off the site or that chert lacking a distinctive cortex, perhaps recovered from local tributary stream beds, may have been used. In the latter instance, primary reduction on site cannot be ruled out. Preliminary examination of the chert indicates that the Burlington formation was used exclusively as the source material. Large pieces of hematite were also recovered from the site.

Despite the presence of diagnostic artifacts found with human burials it would be incorrect to interpret the site as only a cemetery. Five thousand flakes and 1,000 blocky fragments were tabulated for four excavation units. When projected across the entire site it is clear that a substantial amount of lithic reduction is represented. The recovery of manos and the morphological and technological variation represented in the unifacial and bifacial chipped-stone artifacts suggest additional activities occurred at the site. Although an Early Woodland component is present at the site, the diagnostic

Stemmed Bifaces

An examination of the stemmed bifaces indicates a variety of styles (see Appendix A. 1-16). Ten percent of the assemblage is classified as Early Archaic and includes seven distinct styles: Beaver Lake, Kirk, MacCorkle, LeCroy, Thebes cluster, Hardin, and an unnamed corner-notched variety. Sixty-eight percent of the Early Archaic specimens are complete and fifty-eight percent have beveled edges, indicative of reworking.

Middle Archaic specimens account for seventy-five percent of the stemmed bifaces. The most numerous are Osceola (n=80) followed by Godar (n=74) and Matanzas (n=69). Eighty percent are complete and fifty-seven percent have been reworked. The two Late Archaic Kampsville Barbed stemmed bifaces account for less than one percent of the assemblage. In addition, three Early Woodland contracting stem bifaces were recovered from the site surface.

Bannerstones

Twenty-nine bannerstones have been recorded from the site. These include 28 recovered during the amateur excavations and one from the 1984 CAA excavations. All but four were found below the plowzone. Seventeen appear to be manufactured from nonlocal banded slate. The remaining 12 bannerstones were probably manufactured from locally available igneous material. Five bannerstone types are represented. The most prevalent type is the double-edged or shuttle bannerstone, represented by eleven specimens. The second most common type (n=7) is the tube bannerstone. This is followed by 2 geniculates, 2 clipped wing, and a single crescent type. The clipped-wing category has not previously been identified in the literature. A more extensive discussion of the bannerstones is provided by Kenneth B. Farnsworth in Part Two of this report.

Axes

Forty-three ground-stone axes are presently recorded from the site. These include 42 recovered during the amateur excavations and an additional axe recovered during the 1984 CAA investigations. Sixty-five percent (n=28) are three-quarter grooved whereas the remaining 35 percent (n=14) are full-grooved. Although some specimens exceed 20 cm in length, the majority, 62 percent, are less than 10 cm long. Additional information on the axes is provided by Farnsworth in Part Two of this report.

Site Chronology

The issue of site chronology is difficult to address. In the absence of radiocarbon dates from the site, a relative chronology must be based on chronologically diagnostic artifacts. At the Bullseye site this includes stemmed bifaces and bannerstones. Ten percent of the stemmed biface specimens can be assigned to the Early Archaic period. Although the proportion of Early Archaic specimens is low compared to the Middle Archaic varieties, it is unlikely they represent earlier artifacts picked up and curated by Middle Archaic peoples. The percentage of Early Archaic stemmed bifaces in reliably dated Middle Archaic contexts is generally quite low or zero. In Horizon 6 at the Koster site there was a substantial quantity of side-notched Middle Archaic stemmed bifaces but no Early Archaic specimens (Michael D. Wiant, personal communication 1985).

The vast majority of stemmed bifaces from Bullseye include a variety of Middle Archaic side-notched specimens almost equally divided among Osceola, Godar, and Matanzas. This Middle Archaic assemblage is different from the Koster Horizon 6 Helton Phase stemmed biface assemblage (Cook 1976). Matanzas stemmed bifaces accounted for 61 percent of the stemmed bifaces, but Horizon 6 also included Karnak, Godar, Osceola, and Helton types. Conrad (1981) has argued that Godar and Osceola stemmed bifaces should not be included in the Helton Phase but are instead indicative of the Hemphill Phase, which is transitional between Helton and Titterington. Resolution of this issue must be deferred until assemblages clearly dominated by Osceola or Godar stemmed bifaces have been radiocarbon dated in the lower Illinois River valley.

Based on a comparison of the Bullseye bannerstones with the chronology established by Kwas (1981, 1982), Farnsworth concluded (see Part Two) that two cultural components may be represented. Crescent, shuttle, and reel-shaped forms are more prevalent between 7400 to 6400 B.P., whereas geniculates, tubes, and saddle-faced forms are more common for the period 5400 to 4400 B.P. However, as Kwas (1981) has noted, many "grey areas" remain within the chronology, and many of the bannerstone types assigned to earlier periods may also have been manufactured during later periods. Thus, it is conceivable that a shorter time period dating to the later Middle Archaic period could be represented by the bannerstones.

Analysis of temporally diagnostic artifacts indicates that the Bullseye site was occupied during both the Early and Middle Archaic periods, with an emphasis on the later part of the Middle Archaic period. Although the excavations have resulted in the recovery of Middle Archaic stemmed bifaces within human graves, no Early Archaic stemmed bifaces have been found in human graves. Nevertheless, certain factors suggest that some of the Early Archaic stemmed bifaces may also be related to mortuary behavior. Because the majority of the Early Archaic stemmed bifaces were below the plowzone, some may have occurred in pits. A large quantity, 68 percent, were complete. Broken specimens exhibited breaks primarily along the basal edge or at the tip. There is no indication that these specimens were discarded as part of the retooling process. Future excavations will need to clarify the contextual issue involving the Early Archaic stemmed bifaces.

The paucity of Late Archaic stemmed bifaces indicates that the site was probably occupied infrequently during the Late Archaic period. In addition to the Archaic deposits, an Early Woodland Black Sand component has been identified. Although Black Sand ceramics extend across the entire site surface, they are clearly concentrated in the northeastern section of the site. This portion of the site has not yielded any diagnostic Early or Middle Archaic artifacts.

It is acknowledged that the site context presently makes it difficult to interpret the Early Archaic component. The Keach School Terrace surface has been exposed for almost 10,000 years and has probably experienced little sediment deposition. If an Early Archaic cemetery is represented, Middle Archaic burials could easily intrude into earlier graves. Similar disturbances are likely within the Middle Archaic component. Future excavations will need to identify additional artifact caches and stylistically distinct artifacts with burials so that a more detailed spatial analysis of stylistic variation among stemmed bifaces and bannerstones can be conducted.

MIDDLE ARCHAIC MORTUARY BEHAVIOR

Analyses of Middle Archaic burials have drawn comparisons between bluff-crest cemeteries and burials recovered from habitation sites (Buikstra 1981, Charles and Buikstra 1983). Buikstra (1981) compared Middle Archaic burials from habitation sites and bluff-crest cemeteries and found that individuals buried in the habitation sites exhibited pathologies that would have prevented them from contributing to the group's economy. Buikstra has interpreted this as a factor in a pattern of differential treatment of the dead during the Middle Archaic.

An interpretation of the Middle Archaic bluff-crest cemeteries was presented by Charles and Buikstra (1983). These bluff-crest cemeteries, represented by sites within the central Mississippi drainage, exhibit little internal structure and emphasize group rather than individual identity. Artifacts and caches are rarely found associated with individuals; there appears to be no spatial segregation of bodies or groups of bodies. Most burials are in large pits containing multiple interments; some pits contain as many as 40 individuals. An exception is the Elizabeth Mound on the bluff crest above the Napoleon Hollow site. Here, four young males were found in a pit with a variety of grave goods suggesting some degree of special treatment (Charles and Buikstra 1983).

Charles and Buikstra (1983) interpreted bluff-crest cemeteries as territorial markers correlated with rising population densities. Whether this emphasis on bluff-crest burials beginning at approximately 6 000 B.P. is the result of a change in ritual or in preferred location, the establishment of these prominent markers is interpreted as indicating competition between adjoining economic groups.

The burials at the Bullseye site provide an additional perspective into Middle Archaic and potentially Early Archaic mortuary behavior. In contrast to previous examples, the site appears to represent a large formal cemetery not situated on a bluff crest. In addition, individual burials and grave offerings may be present. The broader issues raised by the burials at the Bullseye site include the following:

1. If the Bullseye site represents a cemetery of extended duration beginning in the Early Archaic and continuing into the late Middle Archaic period, then our concept of Early Archaic utilization of the floodplains may need to be expanded.

2. If Middle Archaic bluff-top cemeteries serve as corporate group territorial markers, then what is the symbolic function of the large floodplain cemeteries?

3. Are the individuals buried at Bullseye representative of the entire population or is only a narrower segment represented?

4. Is the large number of potential grave offerings, represented by stemmed bifaces, bannerstones, and axes, being presented to a corporate group or are they associated with individuals and perhaps indicative of an increasingly complex social organization that may involve individual status recognition?

SUMMARY

The results from the Bullseye site excavations are only preliminary. Artifact analysis is not completed and excavations are continuing. However, it is evident that the site can provide important information on technology, settlement, health, and social organization during the Middle Archaic and potentially the Early Archaic periods.

PART TWO: PRELIMINARY EVALUATION OF BANNERSTONES AND OTHER GROUND-STONE ARTIFACTS FROM THE BULLSEYE SITE, 11-Ge-127.

by
Kenneth B. Farnsworth

INTRODUCTION

Although the term "preliminary" is badly overused by archaeologists cautious about making final interpretive pronouncements from their data, it is clearly appropriate for the present report. This study of ground-stone artifacts collected by Jim Wear from the Archaic cemetery area of the Bullseye site has been conducted through the volunteer efforts of Marvin Jeter, Harold Hassen, and myself. As is usually the case with such spare-time activities, the evaluation is far from complete. Studies of these artifacts in their regional context will continue, and eventually a more comprehensive report will be published. Nonetheless, it is appropriate to provide a descriptive progress statement because the Wear family's discovery of the Bullseye site cemetery and its bannerstone assemblage was a primary impetus for funding of professional excavations at the site by the Corps of Engineers.

Ground-stone artifacts in Jim Wear's collection as of June 1984, fall into four categories:

1) bannerstones (28 whole and fragmentary examples);
2) grooved axes (14 full-grooved and 28 three-quarter examples);
3) drilled plummet (1 example);
4) tubular pipe (1 example).

Each of these four artifact classes will be discussed. All except five small bannerstone fragments are illustrated in the Appendix (Figures A.17-31). Metric data not obvious from the photographs are available on request. This report focuses on the chronological implications of Bullseye site ground-stone artifact styles for determining the age of the mortuary facility. In addition, observations are presented on associated attributes of bannerstone styles and trade interaction implied by the presence of the banded slate forms.

Data on lower Illinois Valley regional distribution of sites such as the Bullseye cemetery and distributions of similar bannerstone styles known from the area are given only cursory attention because data-gathering for this aspect of the study is still underway. Also, no detailed technological study has yet been undertaken to identify the lithic raw materials used in bannerstone manufacture although the classic upper Great Lakes banded-slate specimens are obvious. Some of the specimens are not completely drilled, but there is no evidence for bannerstone manufacture at the Bullseye site (in the form of fragments of similar raw material or drilled shaft cores) so it will be assumed that they were brought to the site and included in the cemetery in the form discovered.

Finally, it is not the purpose of this study to debate the function of bannerstones. Whether or not some or all of them functioned as atlatl weights is still an open question (cf. Kwas 1982). The Bullseye site data set provides no new information to resolve this issue.

ARTIFACTS

The Wear Collection Bannerstones

Table 1 lists the attributes of bannerstones found by the Wear family. Four of the artifacts were found on the ground surface immediately above the cemetery area after deep plowing; the remainder were excavated from the cemetery. Four tiny indeterminate fragments are not listed or illustrated. Three of these are banded slate whereas the fourth is limestone (possibly a fragment of no. 9). Number 24 is listed only tentatively. It is a slightly modified, naturally crescent-shaped, brownish-gray sandstone cobble, which may, in fact, be simply a hammerstone. The remaining 23 bannerstones can be grouped into five basic shapes (terminology primarily from Knoblock 1939 and Kwas 1981):

1) crescent;
2) "clipped wing";
3) geniculate;
4) tube;
5) shuttle/reel;
   (double-edged, winged).

The single banded slate crescent (Figure A.17) has a circular drilled shaft with the exterior surface ridged on one side but concave on the opposite face. As far as is known, the two "clipped wing" (term coined by Jim Wear) bannerstones are a unique form. They are both made of banded slate, and both are nearly identically asymmetrical in outline (Figure A.17). They are saddle faced with contracting sides. Both have drilled shafts that are rectangular in outline, formed by drilling two partially overlapping circular holes and then gouging out the ridge that remains. These two bannerstones were found together and perhaps were associated with the same burial. Fragments of a third, nearly identical "clipped wing" bannerstone (also made from banded slate) were recovered by CAA excavators nearby in Test

Square 1 (see Part One, Figure 5). The two banded-slate, L-shaped, geniculate bannerstones were also found side by side and again may have been buried together. They, too, are similar in shape (Figure A.18) although one has a squared toe whereas the other comes to a bladelike edge. The oval-shaped shafts appear to have been drilled as circular holes and then expanded laterally by grinding.

The site has yielded seven tube-shaped bannerstones. Six of these were finished specimens (five of banded slate; one of limestone) with circular shafts. The seventh is a roughed-out tube of limonite with one slightly flattened side (Figure A.26). Hollow-reed drilling had been started and abandoned at one end (Figure A.21, lower left). Among the six finished specimens, at least five have atypical cross-section shapes: four are saddle-faced and the fifth is concave-backed (Figure A.19 and A.20). The sixth fragment is too small to determine its cross section shape.

The final category of bannerstones from the site is the double-edged winged ("shuttle") shape. These occurred in three basic forms (cf. Figure A.22):

1) reel-shaped;
2) contracting-winged with concave top and bottom surfaces;
3) contracting or tapered winged with ridged shafts.

The two reel-shaped bannerstones not only have concave top and bottom surfaces, but have concave sides as well (Figure A.22, top right; Figure A.23, far right). Both are banded slate and both have rectangular shaft drilling like that used for the "clipped wing" types described above. Two contracting-winged shuttles also have concave top and

Table 1. Attributes of bannerstones in the Jim Wear Collection from the Bullseye Site.[1]

No.	Type	Morphology Notes	Raw Material	Figure No.	Drilling
1	Crescent	ridged/concave shaft	banded slate	A.17 left	circular
2	"Clipped Wing"[2]	both are an assymetrical saddle-faced	banded slate	A.17 upper right / A.21 upper right	rectangular
3	"Clipped Wing"[2]	variant w/contracting sides	banded slate	A.17 lower right / A.21 lower right	rectangular
4	Geniculate[2]	L-shaped, blunt toe	banded slate	A.18 left	oval
5	Geniculate[2]	L-shaped, sharp toe	banded slate	A.18 right	oval
6	Tube	saddle-faced	banded slate	A.19 top / A.21 upper left	circular
7	Tube (2/3 fragment)	saddle-faced	banded slate	A.20 lower left	circular
8	Tube (1/3 fragment)	saddle-faced	banded slate	A.20 lower right	circular
9	Tube (2/3 fragment)	saddle-faced	limestone	A.20 top / A.21 top center	circular
10	Tube	concave-back	banded slate	A.19 bottom / A.21 bottom center	circular
11	Tube (indeterminate: split mid-section fragment)	———	banded slate	———	circular
12	Tube	flat-back	limonite	A.21 lower left / A.26 upper right	circular (started but unfinished)
13	Reel	double edged rectangular with concave sides and concave top/bottom surfaces	banded slate	A.22 upper right	rectangular
14	Reel		banded slate	A.23 far right	rectangular (?)
15	Shuttle	double-edged contracting winged w/excurvate sides and concave top/bottom surfaces	banded slate	A.22 upper left	rectangular
16	Shuttle		banded slate	A.23 right center	oval
17	Shuttle[3]	double-edged contracting winged with ridged shaft	banded slate	A.22 bottom	circular
18	Shuttle[3] (1/2 fragment)		banded slate	A.23 left center	circular
19	Shuttle[3] (1/2 fragment)	double-edged wing w/ridged shaft	fine-grained greenish-gray (shale?)	A.23 far left	circular
20	Shuttle	double-edged contracting wing with ridged/concave shaft	fine-grained blue-gray stone (from local glacial till deposits?)	A.24 center top / A.24 upper right	circular
21	Shuttle	double-edged contracting winged w/ridged shaft		A.24 center bottom / A.24 lower right	circular (started but unfinished)
22	Shuttle[4]	———	———	A.24 upper left	circular (started but unfinished)
23	Shuttle?	double-edged rectangular, roughed out	mottled fine-grained, greenish-gray (shale?)	A.25 left	circular (started but unfinished)
24	(indeterminate)	slightly modified, crescent-shaped cobble (hammerstone?)	brownish-gray sandstone	A.25 right	———

[1] Four tiny fragments excluded (3 slate, 1 limestone).
[2] The two clipped wing bannerstones were found side by side, as were the two geniculate bannerstones.
[3] All three broken vertically along ridged shaft.
[4] Found with full-grooved axe (cf. Figure A.24).

bottom surfaces and also are of banded slate (Figure A.22, top left; Figure A.23, right center). One of these has rectangular shaft drilling whereas the other appears to be oval.

Six of the seven remaining bannerstones in the Wear collection appear to be contracting- or tapered-wing shuttles with ridged shafts (cf. Figures A.22, A.23, and A.24). All six have circular drilling, although in three cases it is incomplete. In this shape category a wide range of raw materials was used. Two are banded slate (drilling complete); three are made of a fine-grained, blue-gray stone, possibly from local glacial till deposits (drilling complete on one only); the tapered specimen appears to be a fine-grained, greenish-gray shale (drilling complete).

The final bannerstone in the collection (no. 23) is only roughed-out and seems destined to have become a double-edged rectangular shuttle. A circular shaft hole has been started in one end (Figure A.25, left). The raw material is a mottled, fine-grained greenish-gray shale.

Several summary observations can be made regarding stylistic and technological attributes of this assemblage:

1) Rectangular or oval shaft drilling occurs only with the two "clipped wing" bannerstones, the two geniculate bannerstones, the two reel-shaped bannerstones, and the two double-edged winged shuttles with concave top and bottom surfaces. All eight of these bannerstones are banded slate.

2) All 15 remaining bannerstones have circular shaft drilling. Six of the seven tubes are completely drilled and one is unfinished; four of six ridged-shaft shuttles are completely drilled; the crescent is completely drilled; and the roughed-out rectangular shuttle is unfinished.

3) All four bannerstones with concave top and bottom surfaces (two shuttles and two reels) have oval or rectangular shaft drilling.

4) All of the 16 banded-slate bannerstones are completely drilled, as is the single limestone example. One of the two greenish-gray shale bannerstones is completely drilled; the other is unfinished. Two of the three fine-grained, blue-gray stone bannerstones have unfinished drilling, as does the sole limonite example and the possible brownish-gray sandstone example. Thus, 100 percent of the banded-slate bannerstones are completely drilled as opposed to 38 percent for those made from other raw materials.

5) The raw material chosen for all bannerstones not made from banded slate seems to have been selected because it was nearly the same color as the slate raw material. The single exception (no. 24) may have been simply a hammerstone.

6) Ridging over large shaft holes seems to present a structural weakness. All three Bullseye site examples made in this way have broken vertically along the ridged shaft.

7) A single saddle-faced surface characterizes four of the five typeable tube bannerstones and both of the "clipped wing" bannerstones. It is also present on the single "clipped wing" fragment recovered by CAA excavators. The "clipped wing"

type is unusual in many of its attributes, but the saddle-face attribute is apparently seldom associated with the more commonly found tube-type bannerstones (cf. Kwas 1981).

Based on the four bannerstone types from Bullseye represented in the previous literature (i.e., crescent, geniculate, tube, and shuttle/reel), two Middle Archaic mortuary components seem to be represented at the site. Kwas (1981) recently presented a summary of dated bannerstone finds and devised a chronology of bannerstone styles. From her chart, Bullseye bannerstones fall into two chronological groups:

> 1) ca. 5500-4500 B.C.
> crescents
> shuttles
> reel-shaped forms;
>
> 2) ca. 3500-2500 B.C.
> geniculates
> tubes
> saddle-faced forms.

For both components, the principal raw material from which bannerstones were manufactured was upper Great Lakes banded slate. Since archaeology has produced no evidence anywhere in the lower Illinois Valley region for local manufacture of banded slate artifacts from imported raw material, it is proposed that these bannerstones were imported into the area as finished objects, which were eventually interred with the dead. The bannerstones in the Bullseye assemblage made from other types of fine-grained slate-colored stone were probably locally produced copies. Since some of this stone is quite hard, it is not surprising that the shaft drilling was left incomplete in several cases. That these incomplete specimens were included with burials certainly suggests that their cere-monial placement with the dead did not require that they be fully functional for their original purpose.

The Wear Collection Grooved Axes

Both full-grooved and three-quarter grooved axes were recovered in quantity by the Wear family excavations at the Bullseye site Archaic cemetery. Full-grooved axes probably first appeared in the lower Illinois Valley region earlier in Middle Archaic times than did three-quarter grooved types (see Griffin 1955, 1968:133), but apparently for most of this period both hafting forms occurred. For instance, Gregory Perino (personal communication) believes that full-grooved axes first appeared in the region by ca. 6000 B.C., but that the three-quarter grooved form may have been present as early as 5000 B.C. Since the axes in the Bullseye assemblage were not found directly in caches with projectile points or bannerstones (except for the single instance where a full-grooved axe and an unfinished double-edged wing shuttle bannerstone occurred together [Figure A.24, left]), little can be said about axe chronology at the site. The fact that a full-grooved axe was found with one of the earlier Middle Archaic bannerstone forms at least does not contradict the expectation that such axes are the earliest Middle Archaic form to appear locally.

The 14 full-grooved and 28 three-quarter grooved axes in the Wear collection from Bullseye are illustrated in Figures A.28 through A.31. If it is assumed that these axes were burial inclusions at the site (pit outlines have long since disappeared around remnant bone fragment scatters) and not discarded from work activity such as clearing the site to establish cemetery areas, then two interesting patterns are apparent:

> 1) Twelve of the three-quarter grooved specimens and four of the full-grooved specimens show evidence of extensive bit

damage from heavy chopping use (see especially Figure A.28). It seems odd that axes important enough to an individual to be included at burial would be so heavily damaged in 38 percent of the recorded cases;

2) Although a few fairly large specimens are present, a significant number of the axes found in the cemetery area are quite small. Twenty-six of 42 (62%) are less than 10 cm in length (see especially Figure A.29).

Miscellaneous Artifacts

The Wears recovered two additional groundstone artifacts from Bullseye in the vicinity of the Middle Archaic cemetery. Both are surface finds.

The first is a "Godar Drilled" plummet made of limonite (cf. Figure A.26; Perino 1961). This plummet type was originally named from specimens found with the type cache of Godar points from the lower Illinois Valley. It is probably contemporary with the later Godar-point Archaic component at Bullseye.

The second is a distinctively styled tubular pipe made of a gray-black steatitelike material (Figure A.26). Tube pipes do not appear in west-central Illinois prior to Terminal Archaic times (ca. 1,500 B.C.), so the Bullseye pipe cannot be associated with either of the site's Middle Archaic components. Although tubular pipes are rare in the lower Illinois Valley region, the two best-documented examples (Braun *et al.* 1982:31-40; Titterington 1947, 1950) were found at Kampsville-mortuary-complex cemeteries established by the area's Terminal Archaic Prairie Lake culture inhabitants (see Farnsworth and Asch 1986). Kampsville Barbed points are another artifact style associated with the Prairie Lake culture in the lower Illinois Valley, and at least two such points have been recovered at the Bullseye site (Figure A.11). Thus the Bullseye site pipe may be associated with a very small Prairie Lake occupation or an isolated Terminal Archaic burial at the site.

However, it should be noted that the two previously known Kampsville-mortuary-complex pipes are simple expanding tubes, whereas the Bullseye pipe is a uniquely flattened, stylized variant. There is an extensive Early Woodland occupation at Bullseye, associated with the regional Cypress phase of the Black Sand culture (Farnsworth and Asch 1986; Hassen, Part One of this report; Hassen and Batura 1983), and the Bullseye pipe perhaps represents an Early Woodland ground-stone artifact style. Because of its distinctive shape, it should be a useful horizon marker for Cypress-phase habitation sites or burials if future studies support this proposed temporal association.

CONCLUSIONS

From the density and distribution of bone fragment concentrations in the Archaic cemetery area at Bullseye site, a projected density of 25 to 50 or more burials in the area would not be unreasonable. Given the quantities of projectile points, drills, axes, and bannerstones found in immediate association with these bone-fragment concentrations throughout the cemetery area, it is apparent that most of the burials were accompanied by grave goods and that these frequently included bannerstones. Caches of projectile points and drills were found in direct contact with each other, but apparently never directly in contact with bannerstones or axes, which were usually found singly. This may simply mean that they were placed on opposite sides of a body when originally deposited in the grave.

Yet with all of these Middle Archaic artifacts and burials at Bullseye, bannerstone finds have been exceedingly rare in the rest of the lower Illinois Valley region. After 25 years of work in the region, Center for American Archeology collections contain less than six whole or fragmentary specimens. Moreover, with the exception of the Godar cache of 24 bannerstones found by a farmer in 1940 (Titterington 1950), few are mentioned in the literature. Nearly 10 years of excavations at the deeply stratified Koster Archaic site (29 km to the south) produced none (Cook 1976, Lurie 1982), although it contained horizons dating throughout the bannerstone-production time span. Perhaps even more surprisingly, recently completed CAA excavations at a blufftop Middle Archaic cemetery found beneath the Elizabeth Mound Group (Charles *et al.* n.d.; Farnsworth and Walthall 1983) yielded only a single crescent bannerstone, a single three-quarter grooved axe, and a few Graham Cavelike points among more than 30 burials. This is certainly a very different pattern of mortuary site artifact disposal than that at the Bullseye floodplain cemetery.

However, recent investigations initiated as the result of the Bullseye project now indicate that at least two similar areas of bannerstone concentrations on floodplain terraces or ridges have been discovered elsewhere by landowners during farming activities. Approx-imately 18 km south of the Bullseye site (just north of Eldred, Illinois) 8 to 10 bannerstones were plowed out in the early 1960s, including a slate crescent and three or four slate tube bannerstones. They have not yet been relocated for study. Also, within the past two years, a farmer in the Mississippi floodplain in Calhoun County plowed out approximately 40 Archaic burials and collected approximately 28 bannerstones from the immediate burial area. The dominant shape is said to be a notched ovate form, and at least one of the artifacts was slate. This collection has not yet been viewed for comparison.

Apparently quite distinct mortuary and habitation site types existed in the region during Middle Archaic times, with the major bluffbase villages and blufftop cemeteries located at a distance from central-floodplain cemeteries. Only minimal habitation acti-vities occurred at the cemeteries, perhaps in association with periods of mortuary ritual. Since the floodplain burials were probably placed deep enough that modern farming activities rarely intersect the graves, an essentially "invisible" site type was created that has not been investigated at all by professional archaeologists prior to our Bullseye site experience.

Bannerstones are not such rare objects as we thought. They were simply rarely left at the types of sites we have studied.

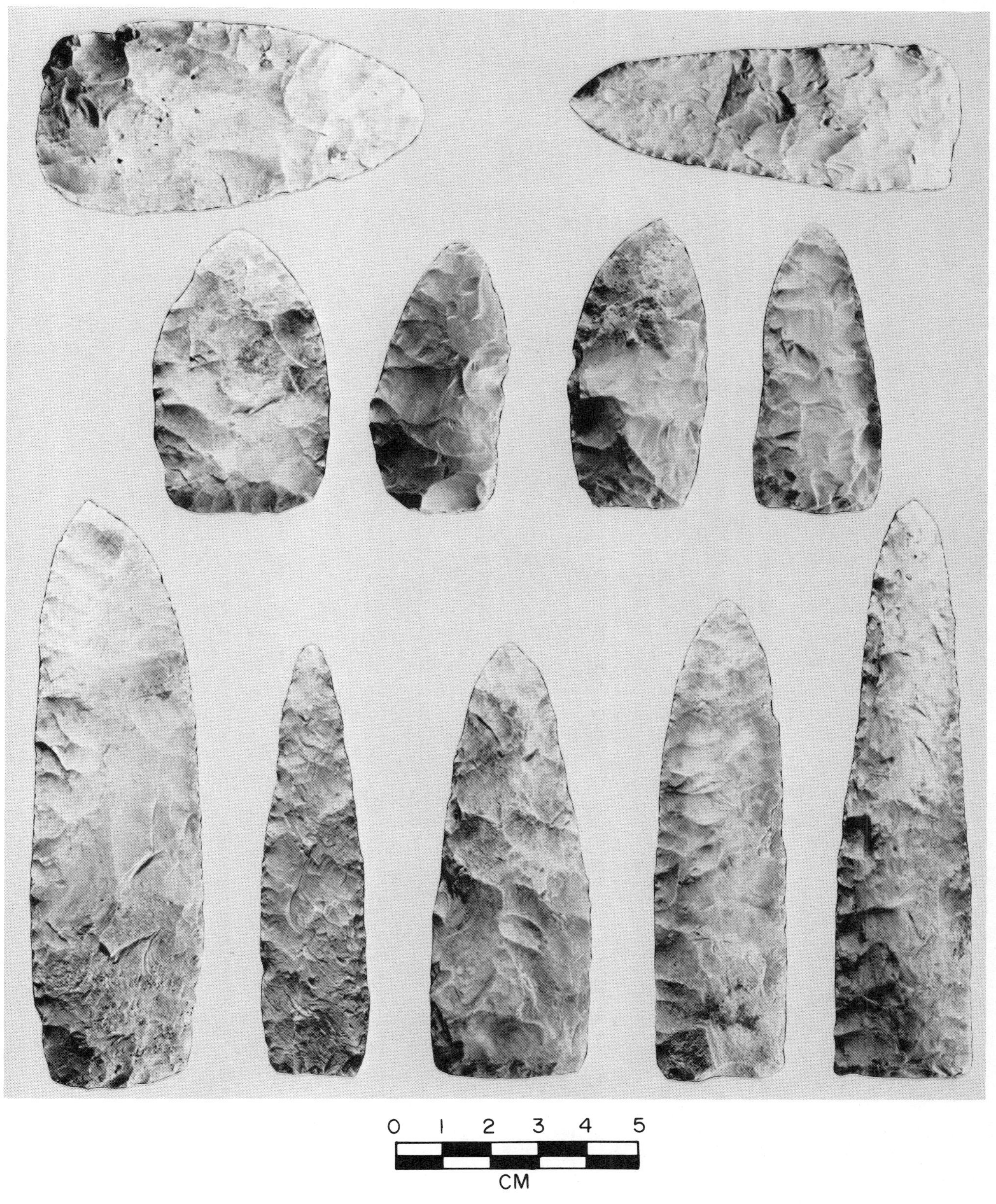

Figure A.1.   Lanceolate bifaces, Bullseye site.

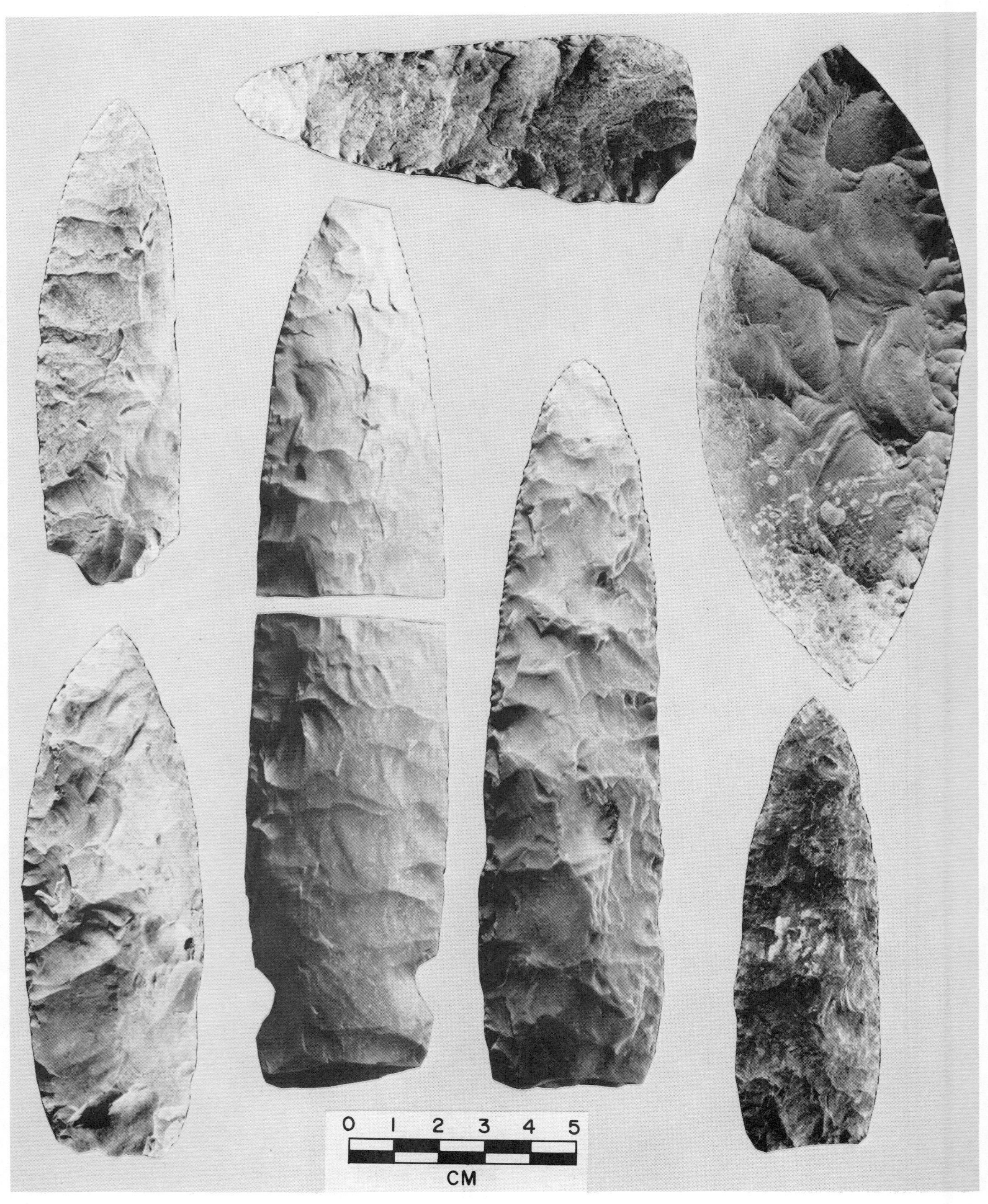

Figure A.2. Assorted stemmed bifaces, Bullseye site.

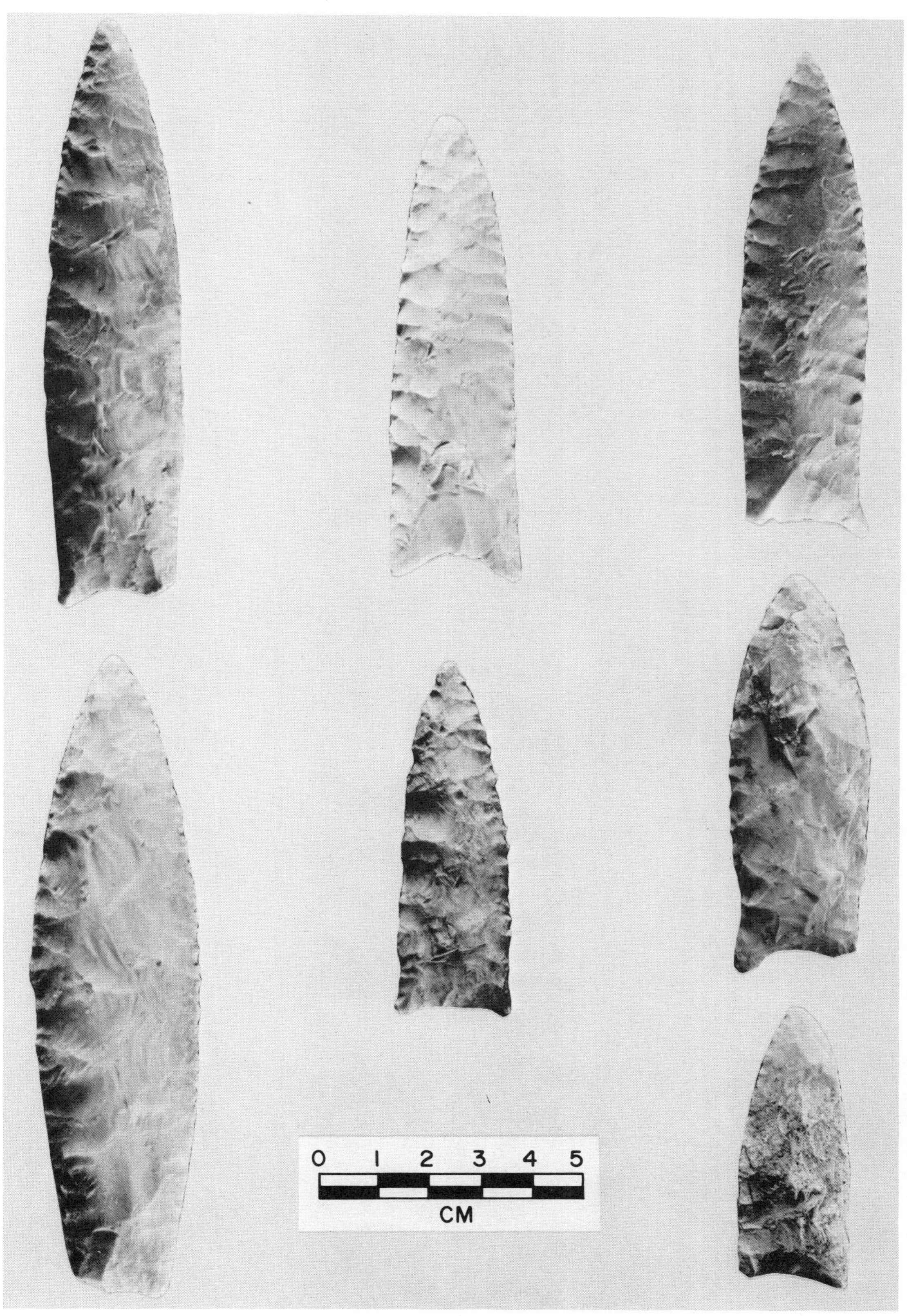

Figure A.3. Lanceolate stemmed bifaces, Bullseye site.

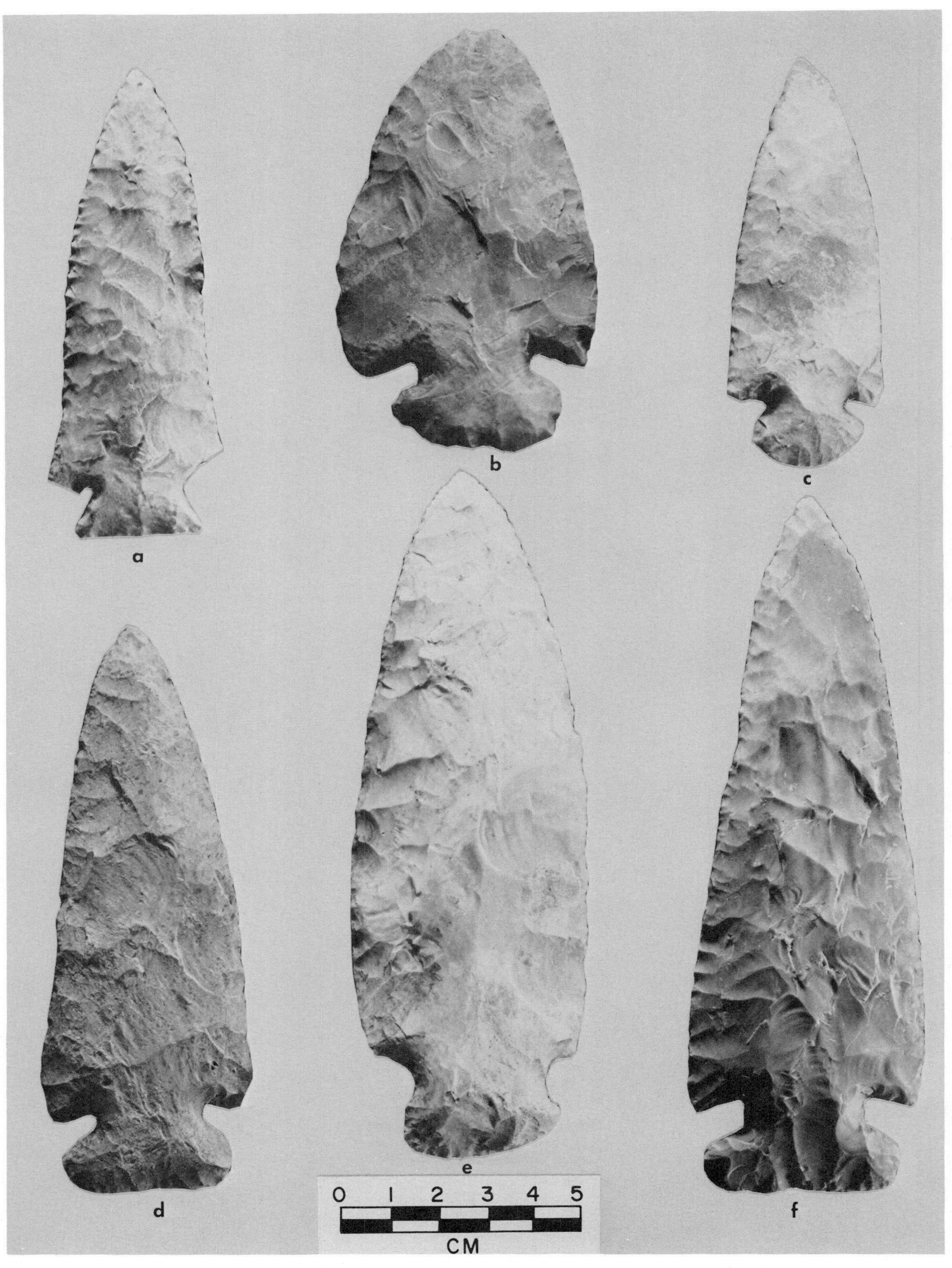

Figure A.4. Stemmed bifaces, Stilwell (a), Thebes (b, d, f), and St. Charles (c), type indeterminate (e), Bullseye site.

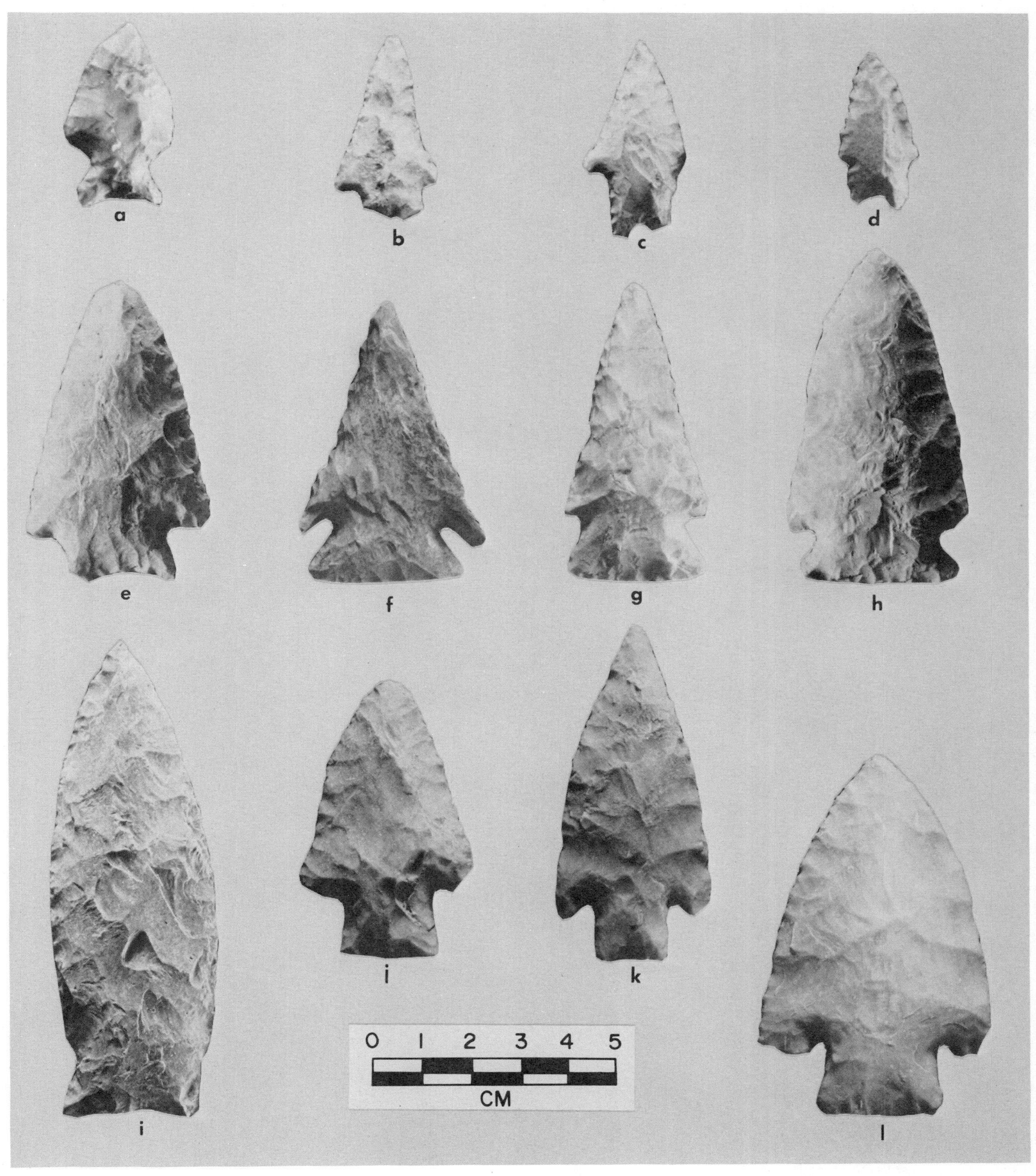

Figure A.5.   Stemmed bifaces, bifurcate base (a, b, c, d), expanding stem (e, g), corner-notched (f), shallow side-notched (h, i), Kampsville Barbed (j, k), and Hardin Barbed (l), Bullseye site.

Figure A.6. Cache 1, amateur excavations (A), cache 2, amateur excavations (B), Bullseye site.

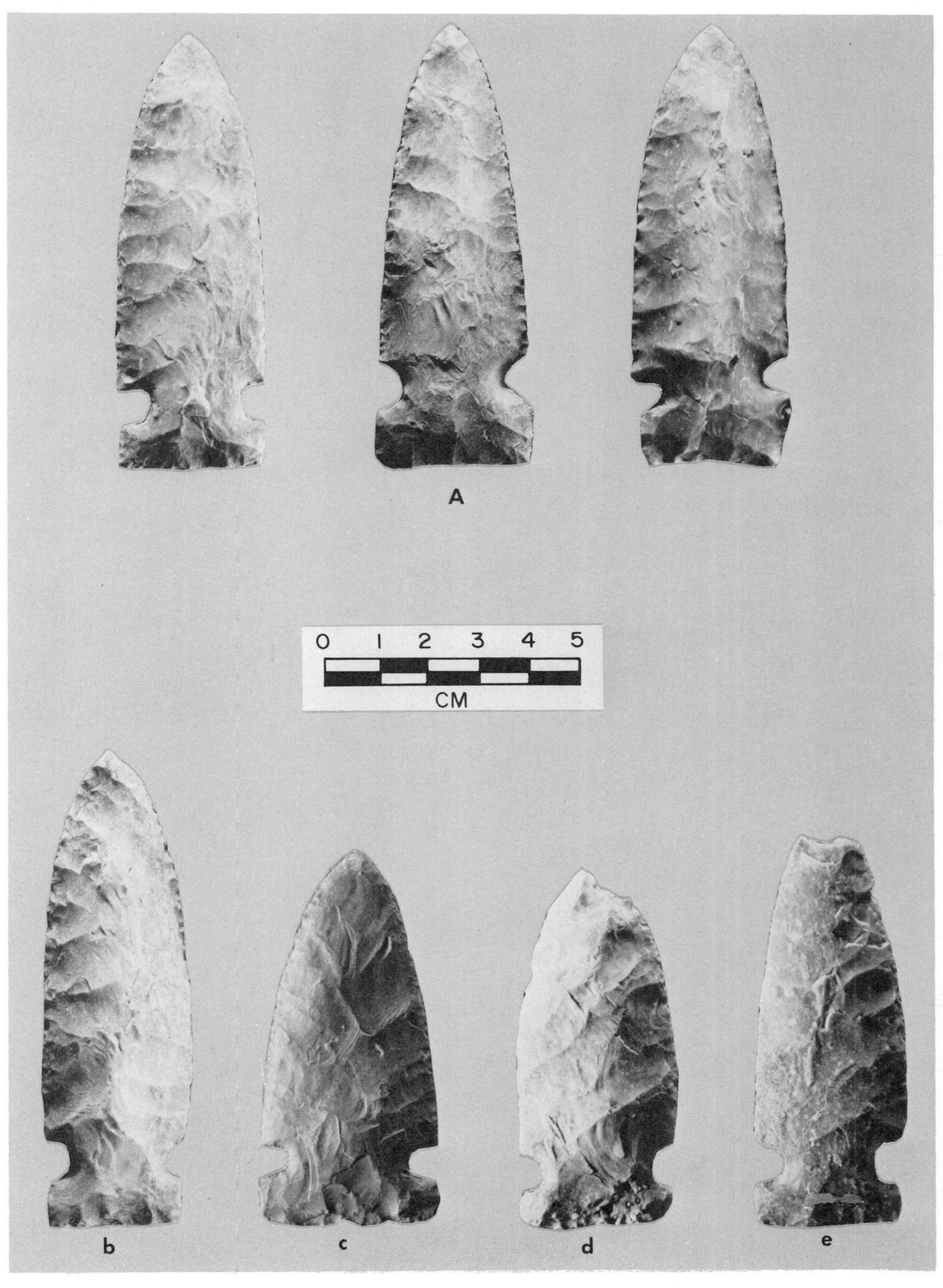

Figure A.7. Stemmed bifaces, side-notched (A, b-e). Cache 3, amateur excavations (A), Bullseye site.

Figure A.8. Stemmed bifaces, side-notched, Bullseye site.

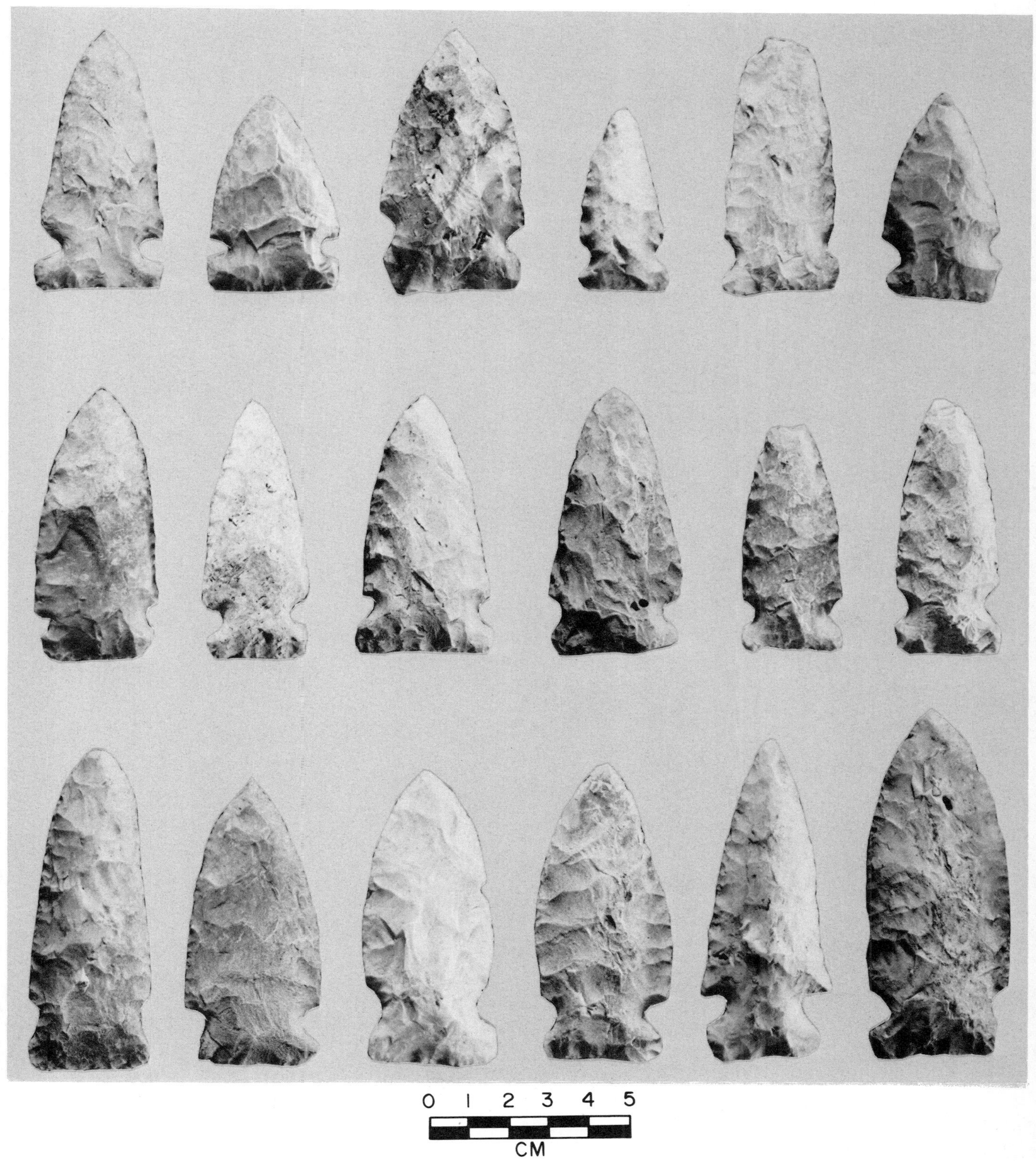

Figure A.9. Stemmed bifaces, side-notched, Bullseye site.

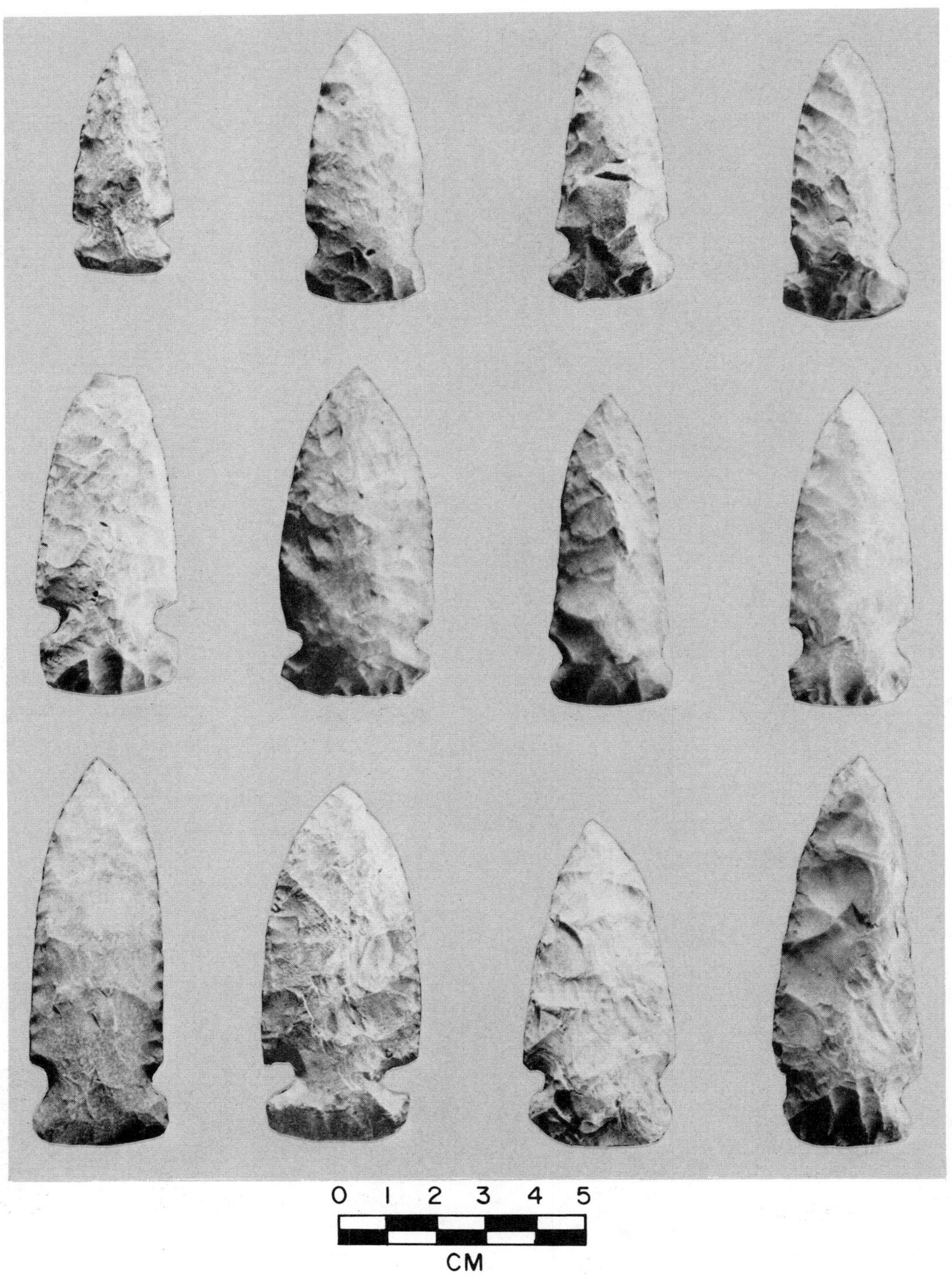

Figure A.10. Stemmed bifaces, side-notched, Bullseye site.

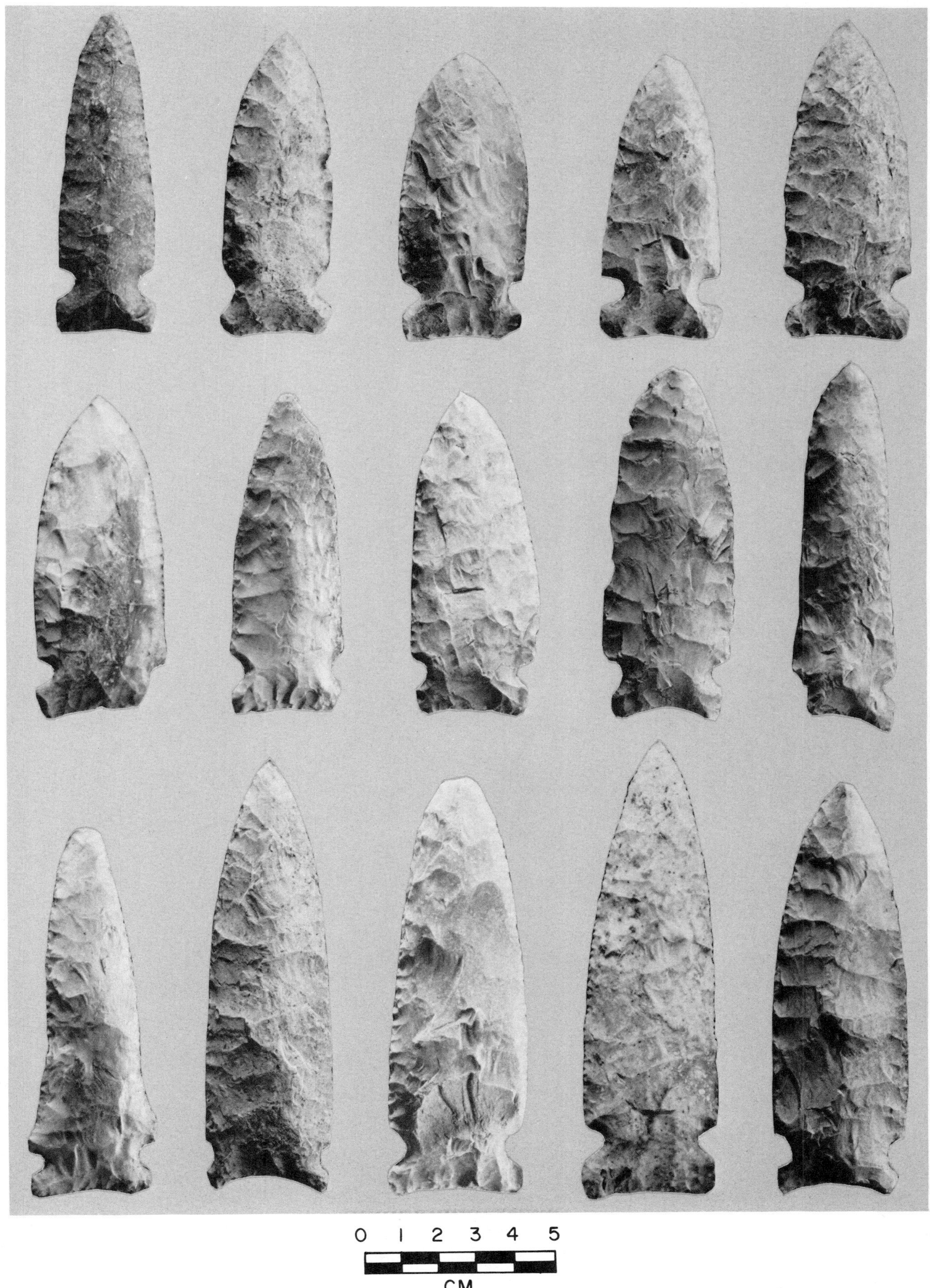

Figure A.11. Stemmed bifaces, side-notched, Bullseye site.

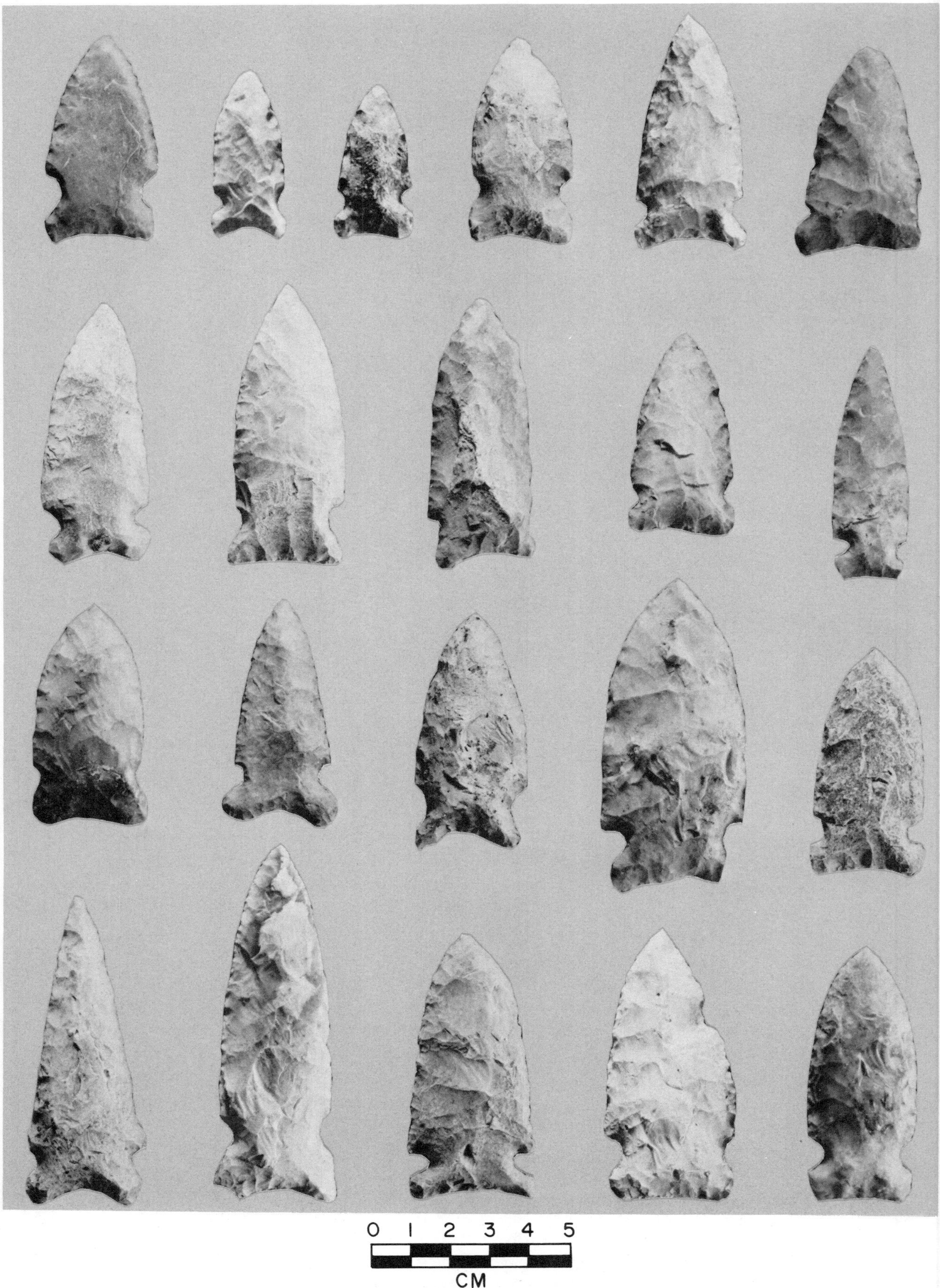

Figure A.12.   Stemmed bifaces, side-notched, Bullseye site.

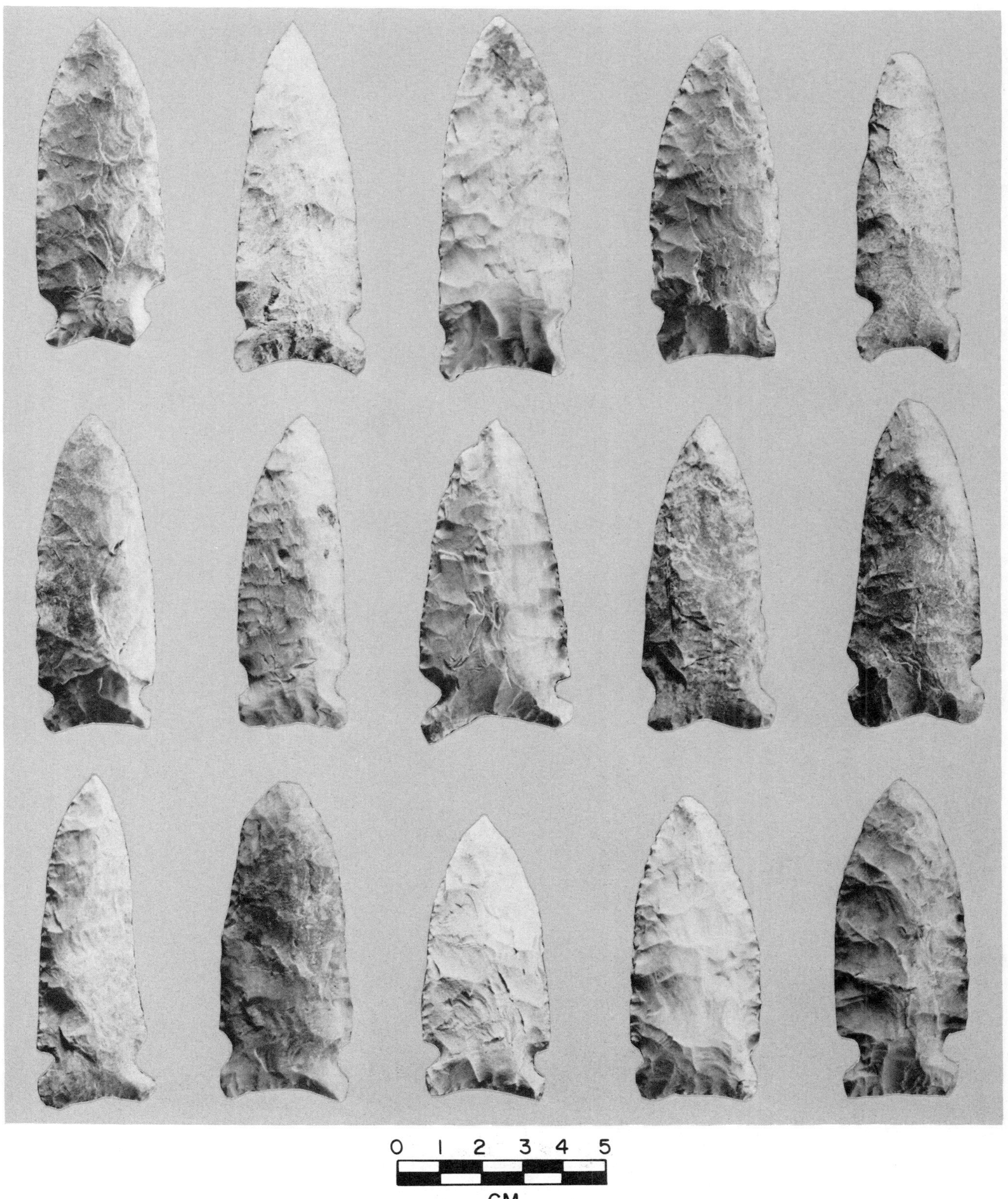

Figure A.13. Stemmed bifaces, side-notched, Bullseye site.

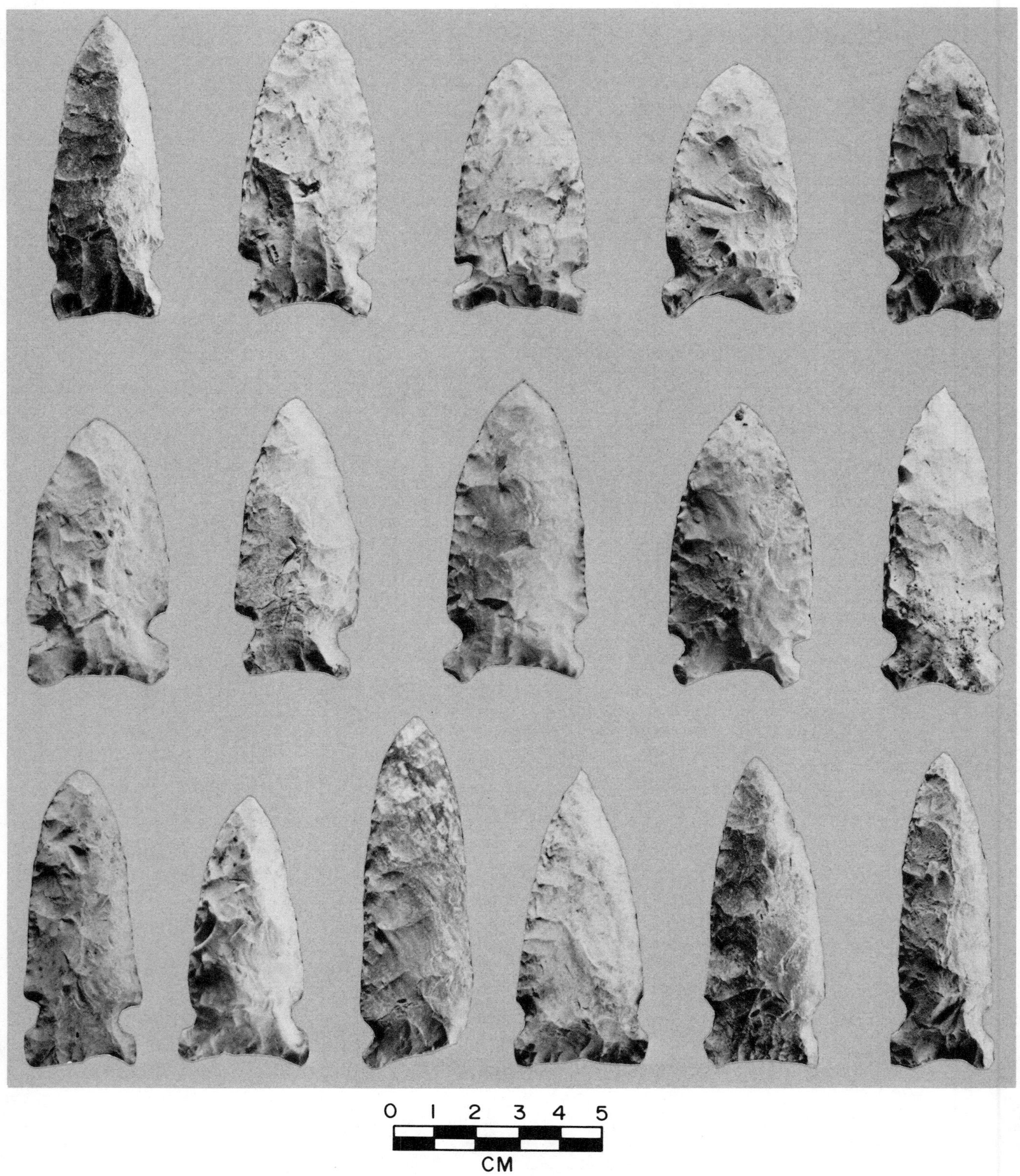

Figure A.14.   Stemmed bifaces, side-notched, Bullseye site.

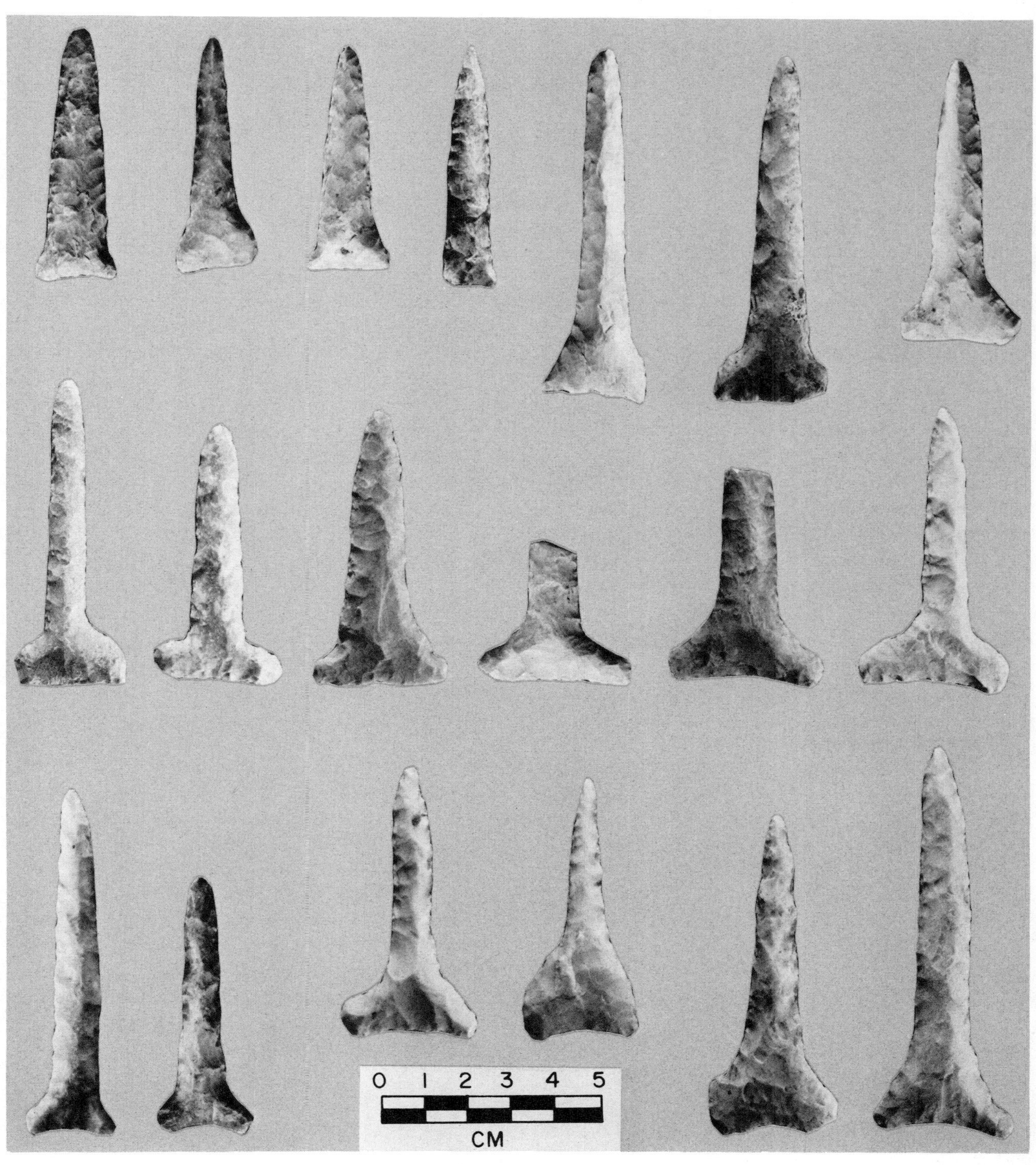

Figure A.15. "T"-shaped drills, Bullseye site.

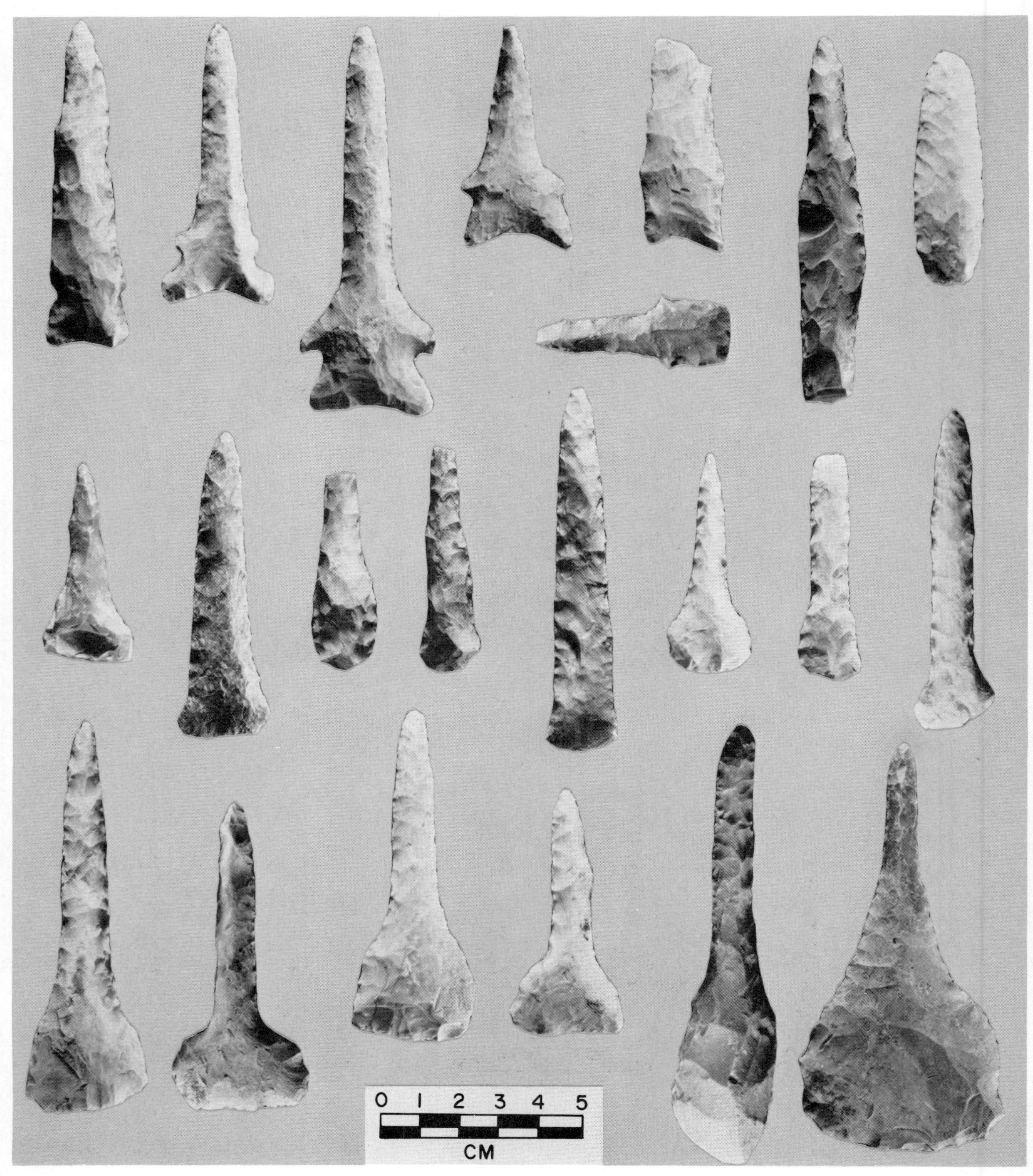

Figure A.16. Reworked stemmed bifaces and drills, Bullseye site.

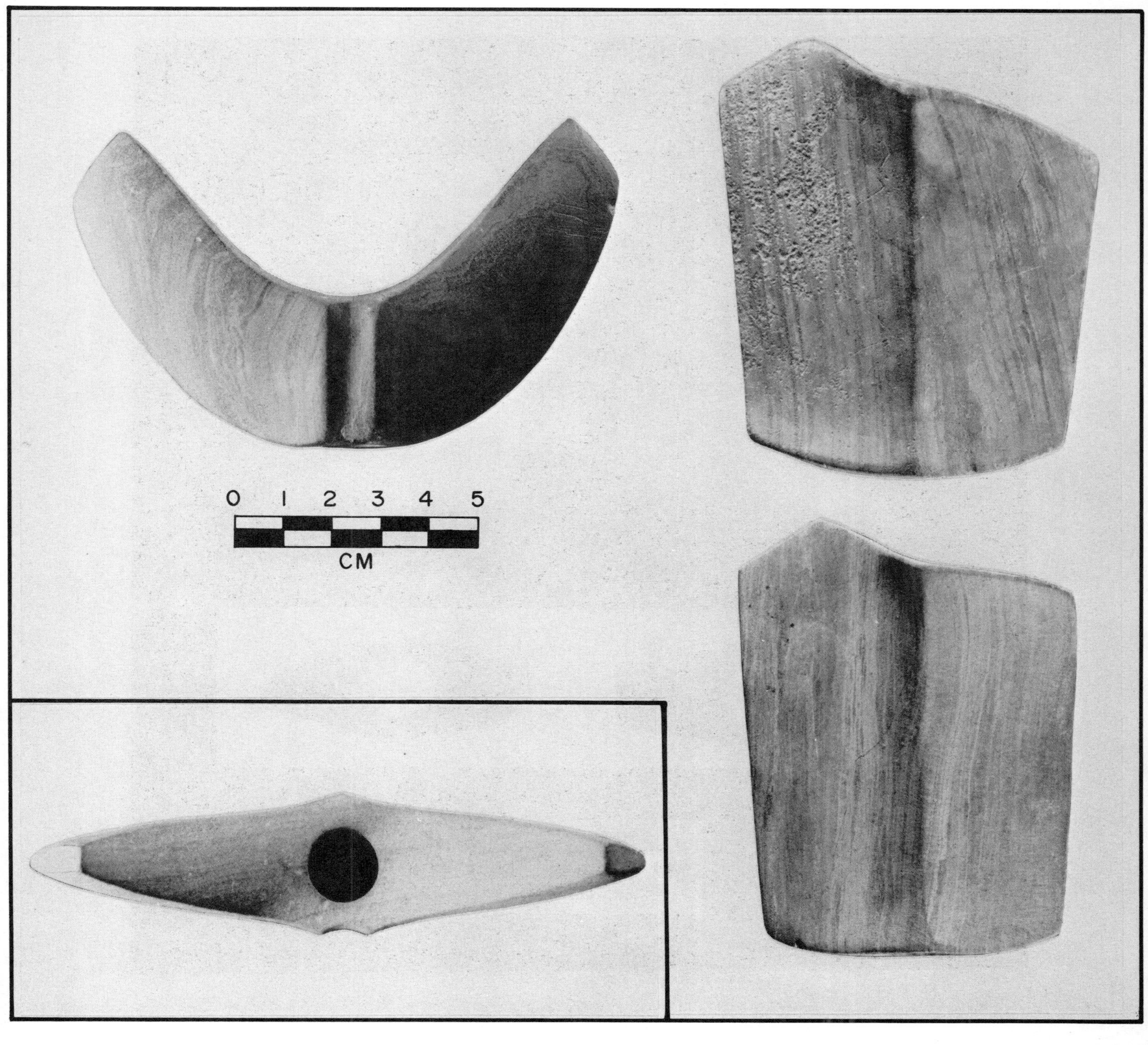

Figure A.17. Crescent bannerstone with ridged/concave shaft, and two asymmetrical, saddle-faced, "clipped wing" bannerstones, Bullseye site. All are banded slate.

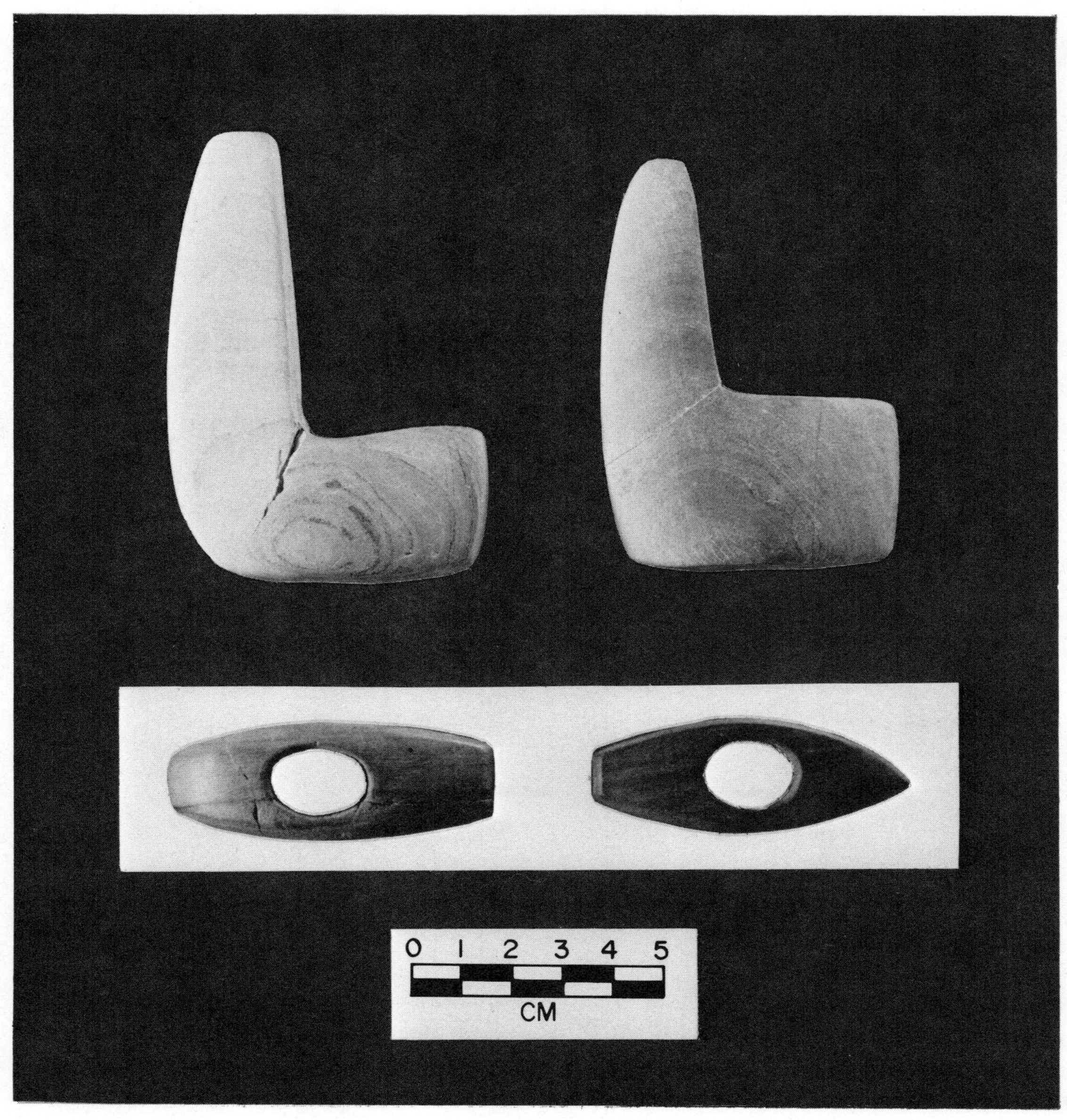

Figure A.18. Geniculate bannerstones found side by side (amateur excavations), Bullseye site. Both are banded slate.

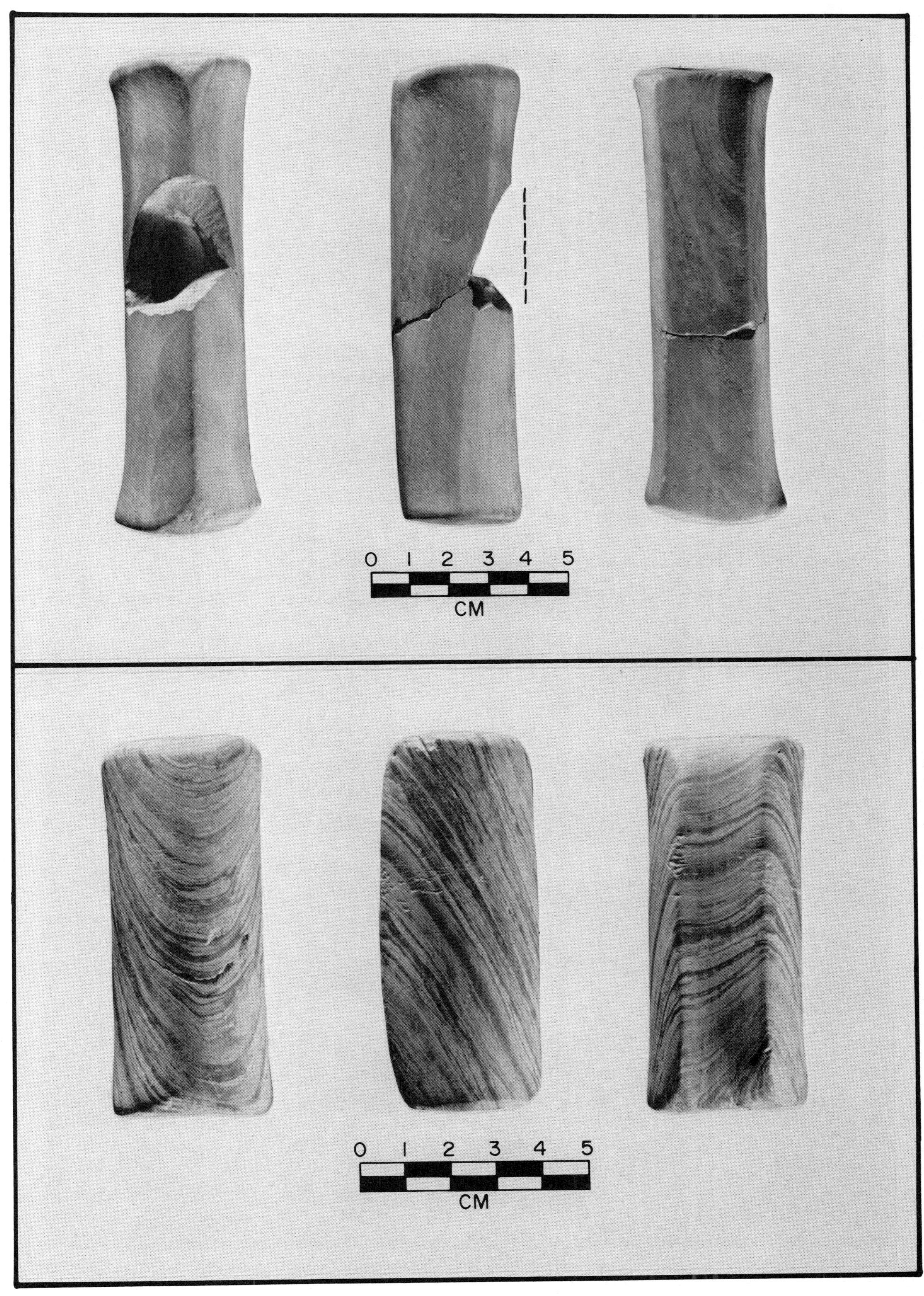

Figure A.19. A saddle-faced tube bannerstone (top) and concave-backed tube bannerstone (bottom), Bullseye site. Both are banded slate.

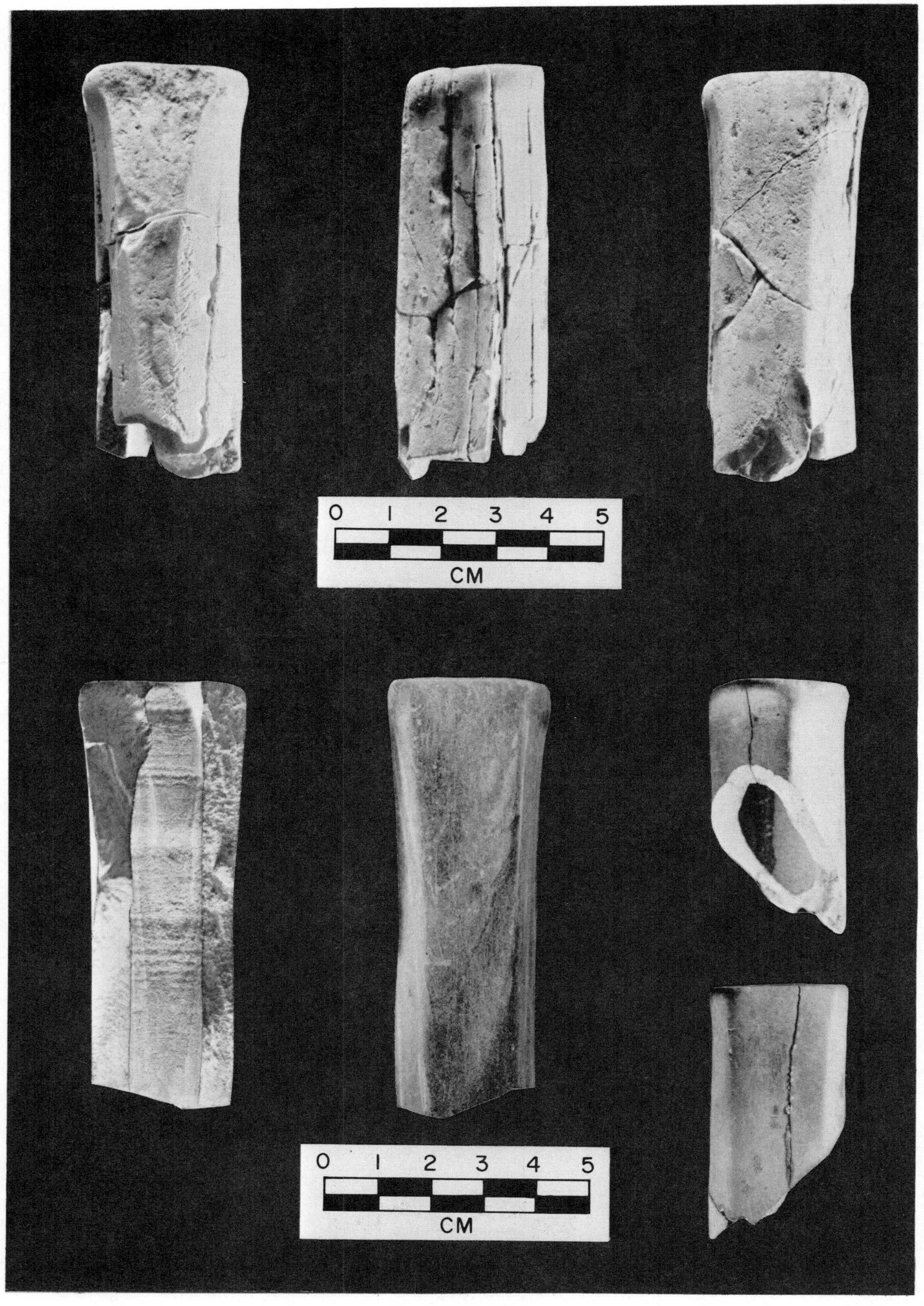

Figure A.20.   Fragments of three saddle-faced tube bannerstones, Bullseye site. **Top** = limestone.   **Lower left** and **lower right** = banded slate.

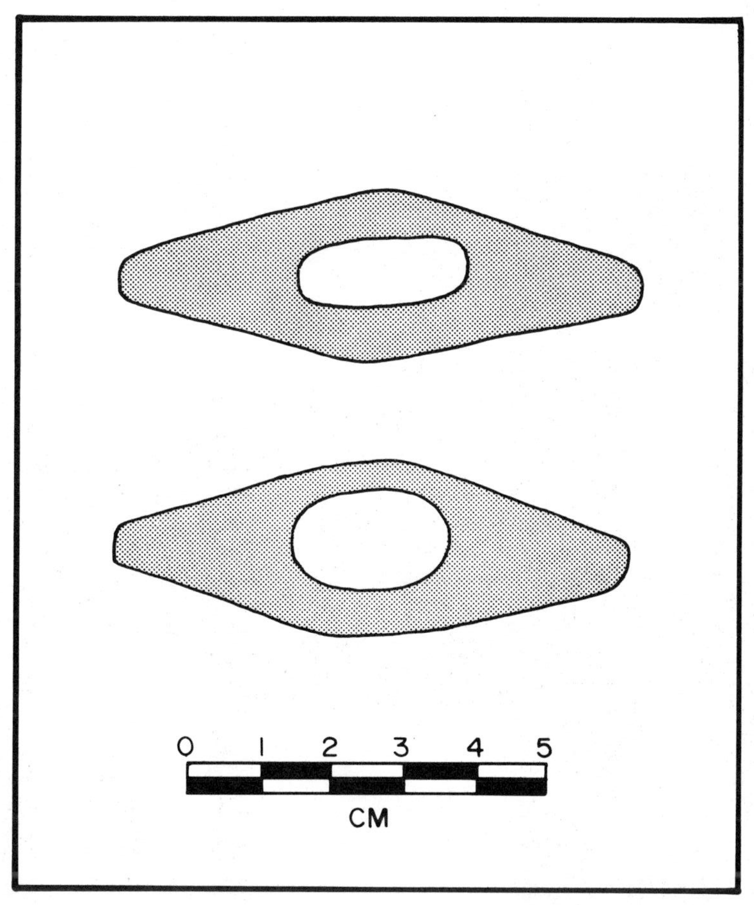
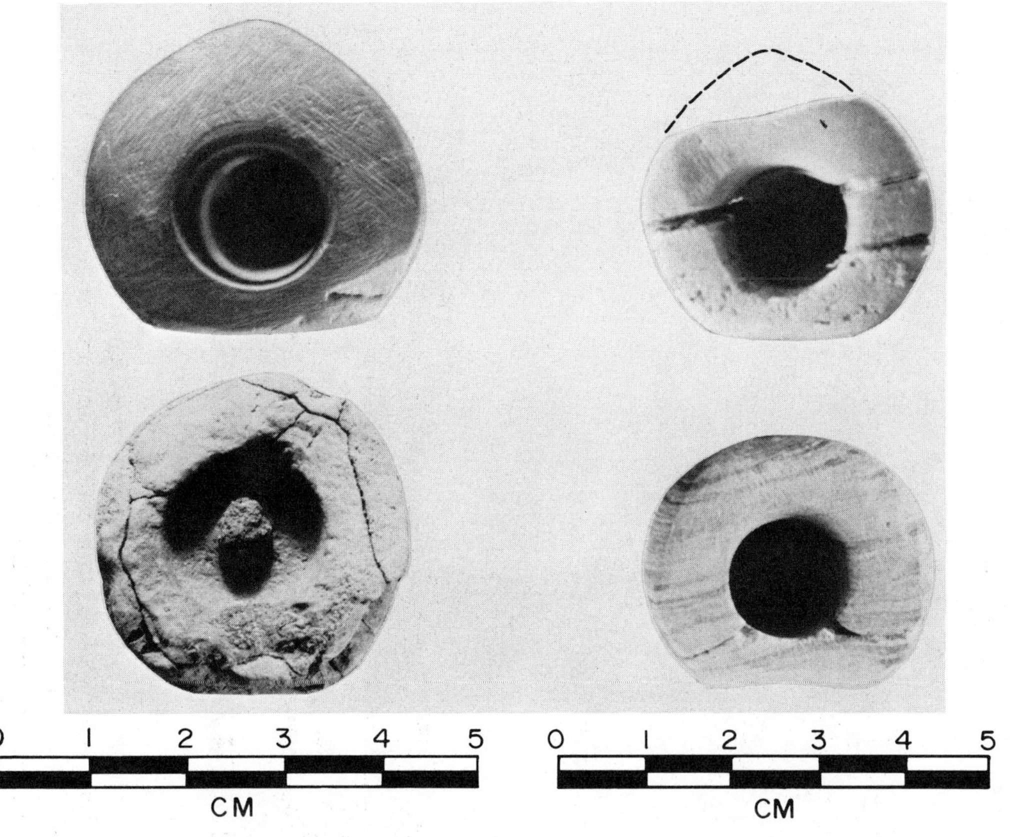

Figure A.21. End views of circular drilling in four tube bannerstones (**left** and **center**) and rectangular drilling pattern in two "clipped-wing" bannerstones (**right**), Bullseye site.

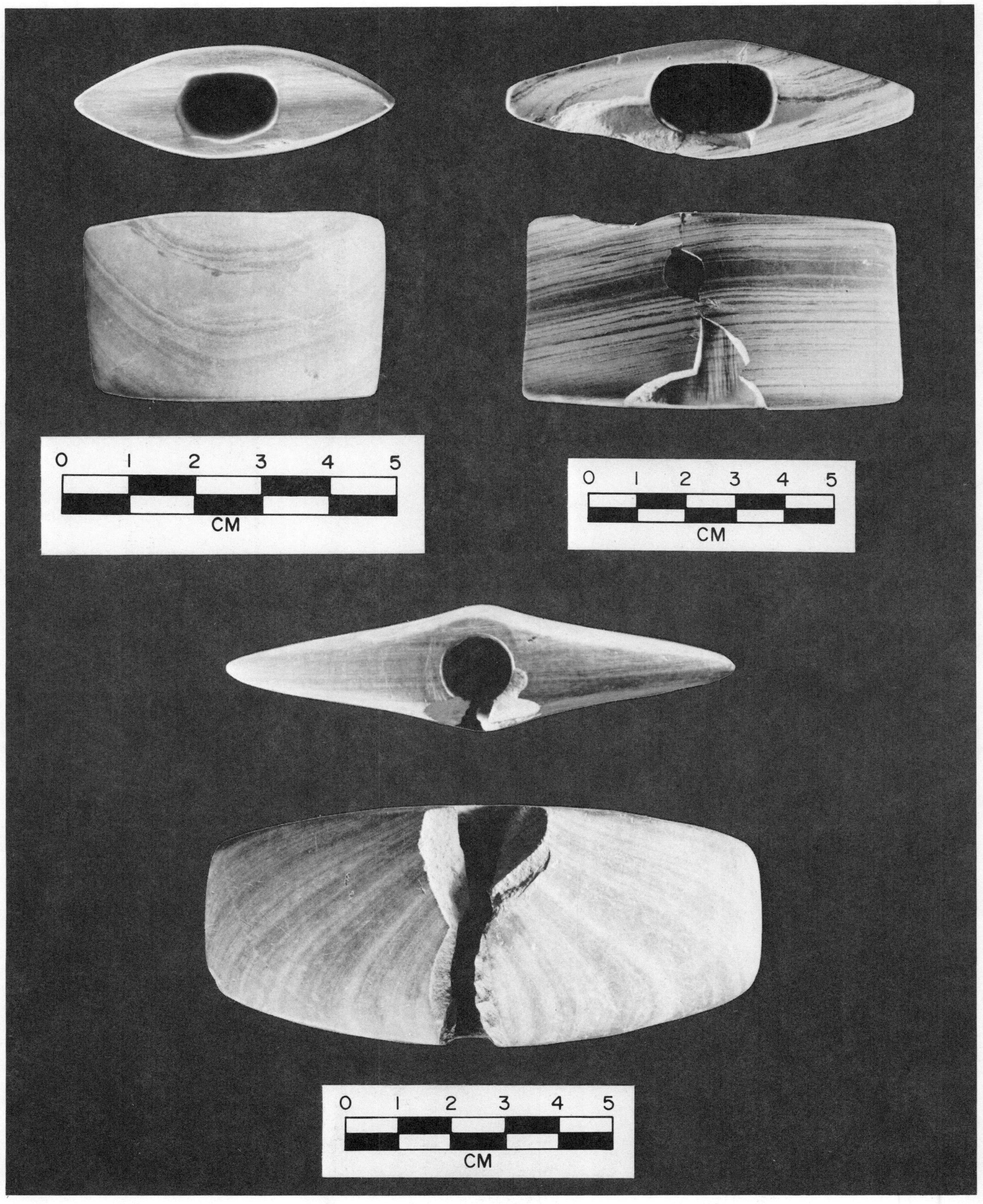

Figure A.22.   Three varieties of simple double-edged bannerstones, Bullseye site.
Upper left = rectangular shuttle, with concave top and bottom faces. **Upper right** = reel-shaped, with all faces concave.   **Bottom** = contracting-wing shuttle with ridged shaft.   All are banded slate.

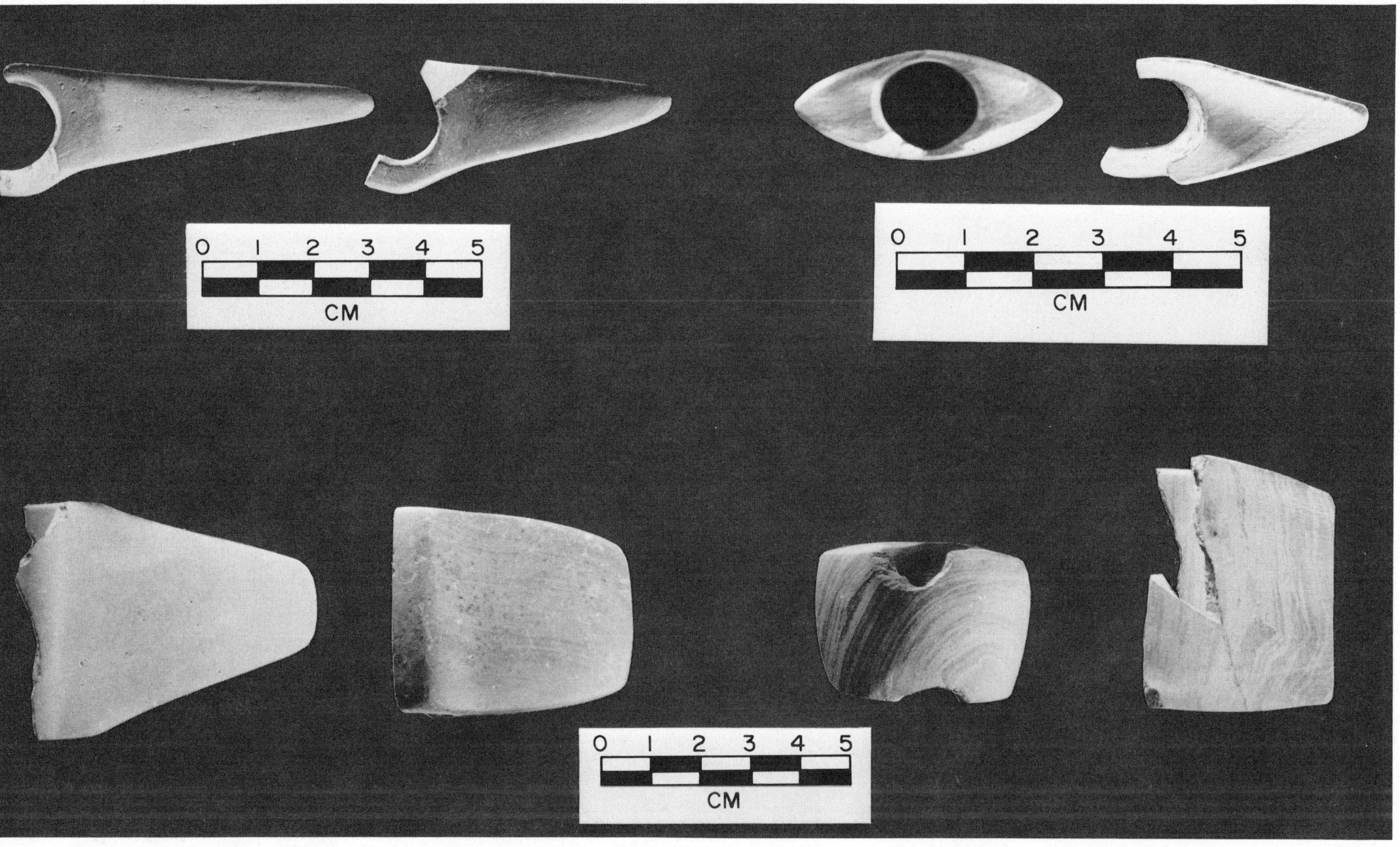

Figure A.23. Additional examples of double-edged bannerstones, Bullseye site. **Far left** = tapered-wing shuttle with ridged shaft. **Left corner** = contracting-wing shuttle with ridged shaft. **Right center** = rectangular shuttle with concave top and bottom faces. **Far right** = reel-shaped, with all faces concave. All are banded slate except far left specimen which is apparently a fine-grained, green-gray shale.

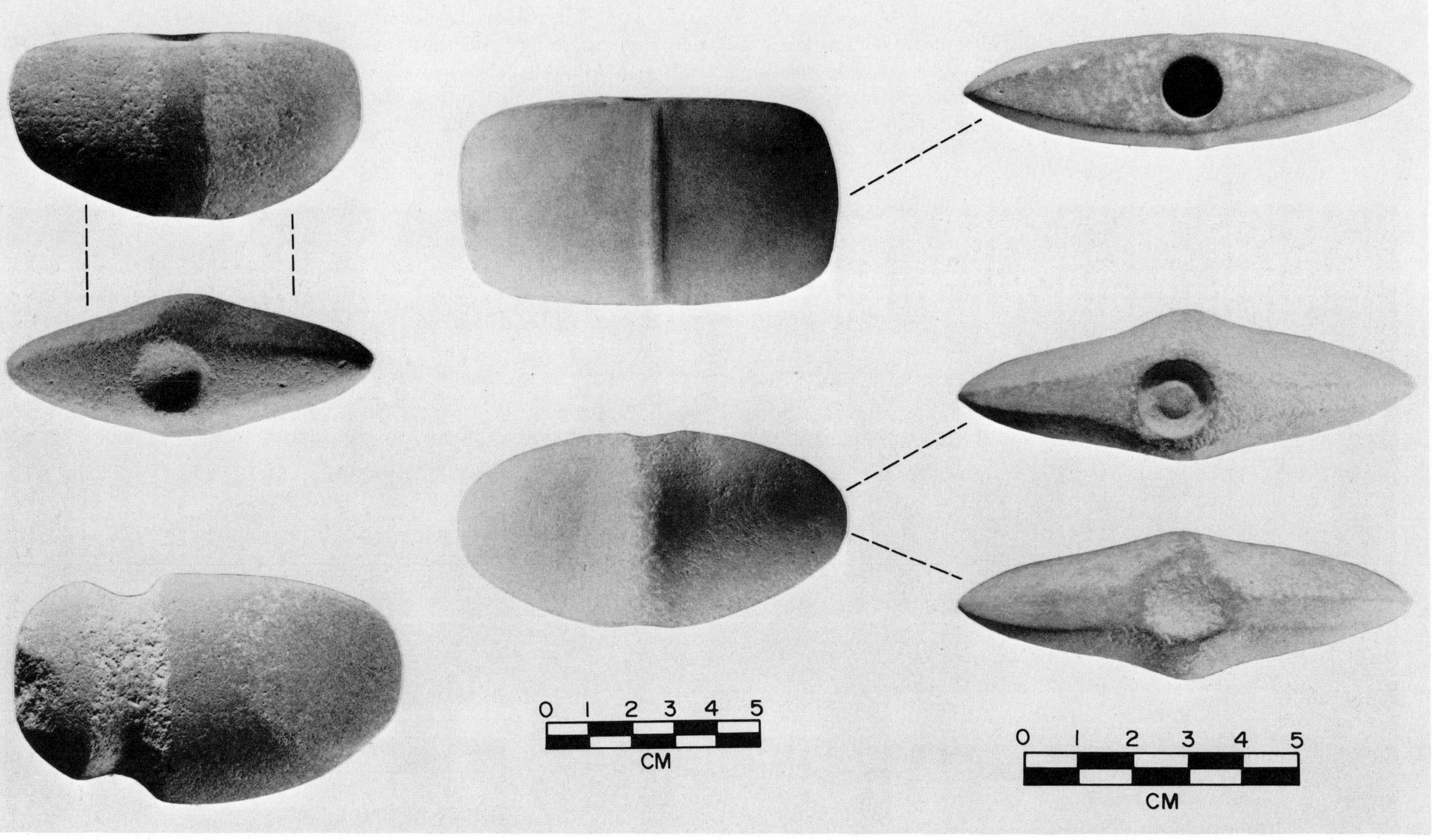

Figure A.24.   Three bannerstones made from a fine-grained, blue-gray stone probably obtained from local glacial till, Bullseye site.   **Left** = unfinished contracting-wing shuttle with ridged shaft (found together during amateur excavations with full-grooved axe shown below).   **Center top** and **upper right** = rectangular shuttle with ridged/concave shaft.   **Center bottom** and **lower right** = contracting-wing shuttle with ridged shaft.

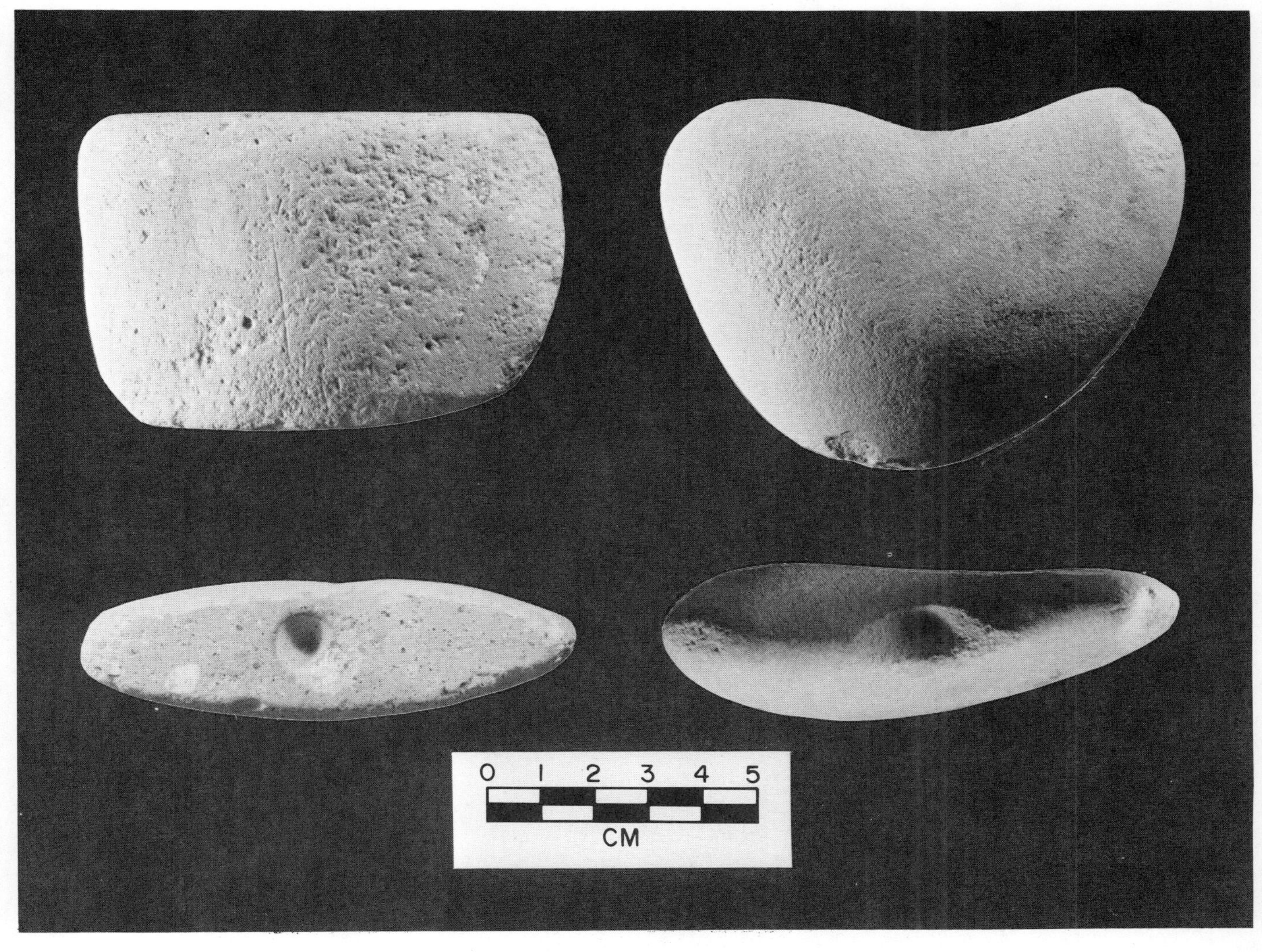

Figure A.25. Two possible roughed-out bannerstones of local raw material, Bullseye site. **Left** = apparent rectangular shuttle of mottled green-gray shale, top drilling started. **Right** = possible roughed-out crescent that is largely an unmodified glacial cobble. Pecked at ends of "wings" and both ends of possible shaft. May be merely a hammerstone. Brown-gray sandstone.

Figure A.26. Miscellaneous ground-stone artifacts, Bullseye site. **Top left** = limonite Godar Drilled plummet. **Top right** = unfinished limonite tube bannerstone with one flattened surface, drilling started at right end. **Bottom** = pipestone (steatite?) tube pipe from the surface near the cemetery. Note gouged interior tube surface.

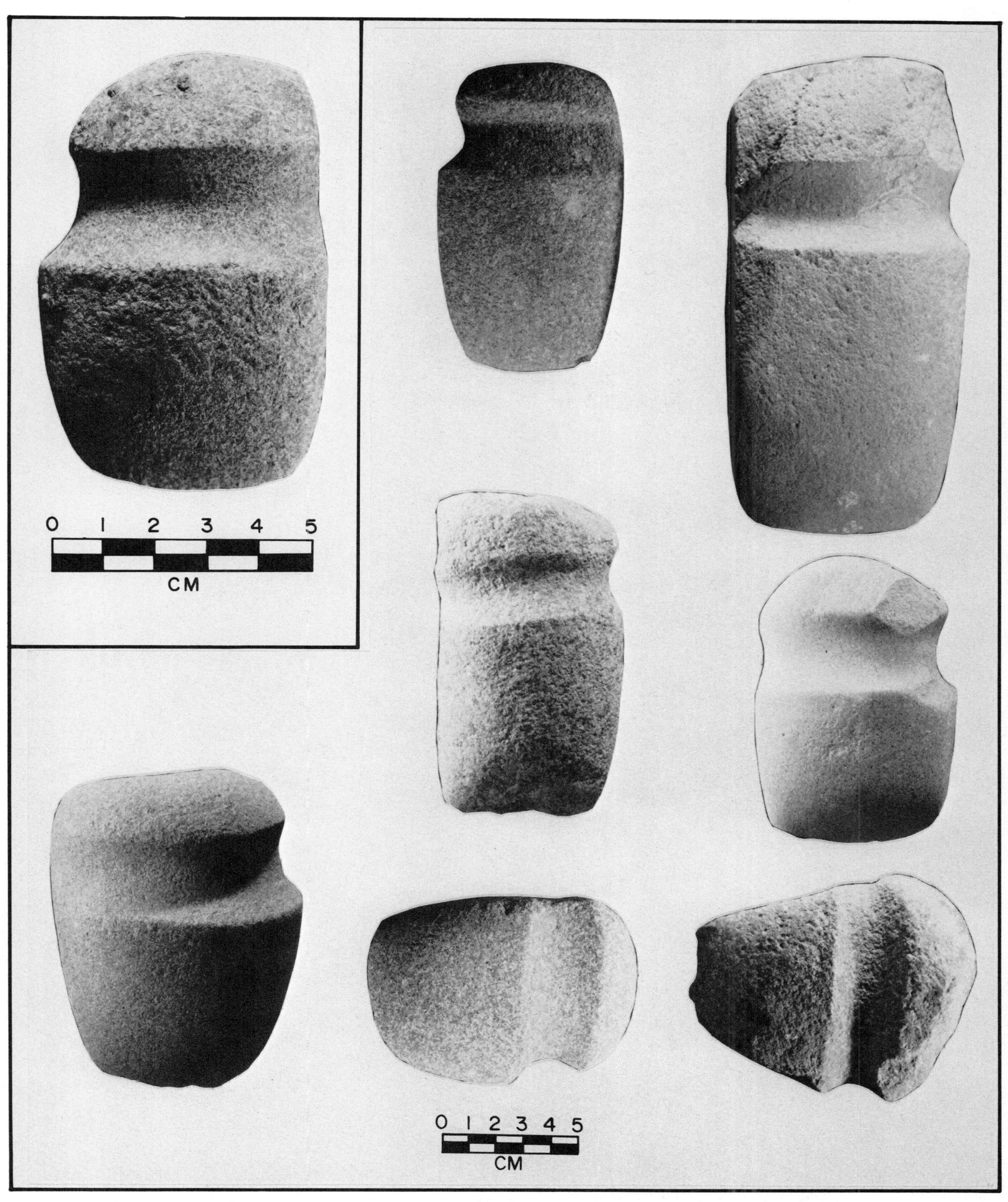

Figure A.27. Three-quarter grooved axes, Bullseye site.

Figure A.28. Large battered three-quarter grooved axes, Bullseye site.

Figure A.29. Small three-quarter grooved axes, Bullseye site.

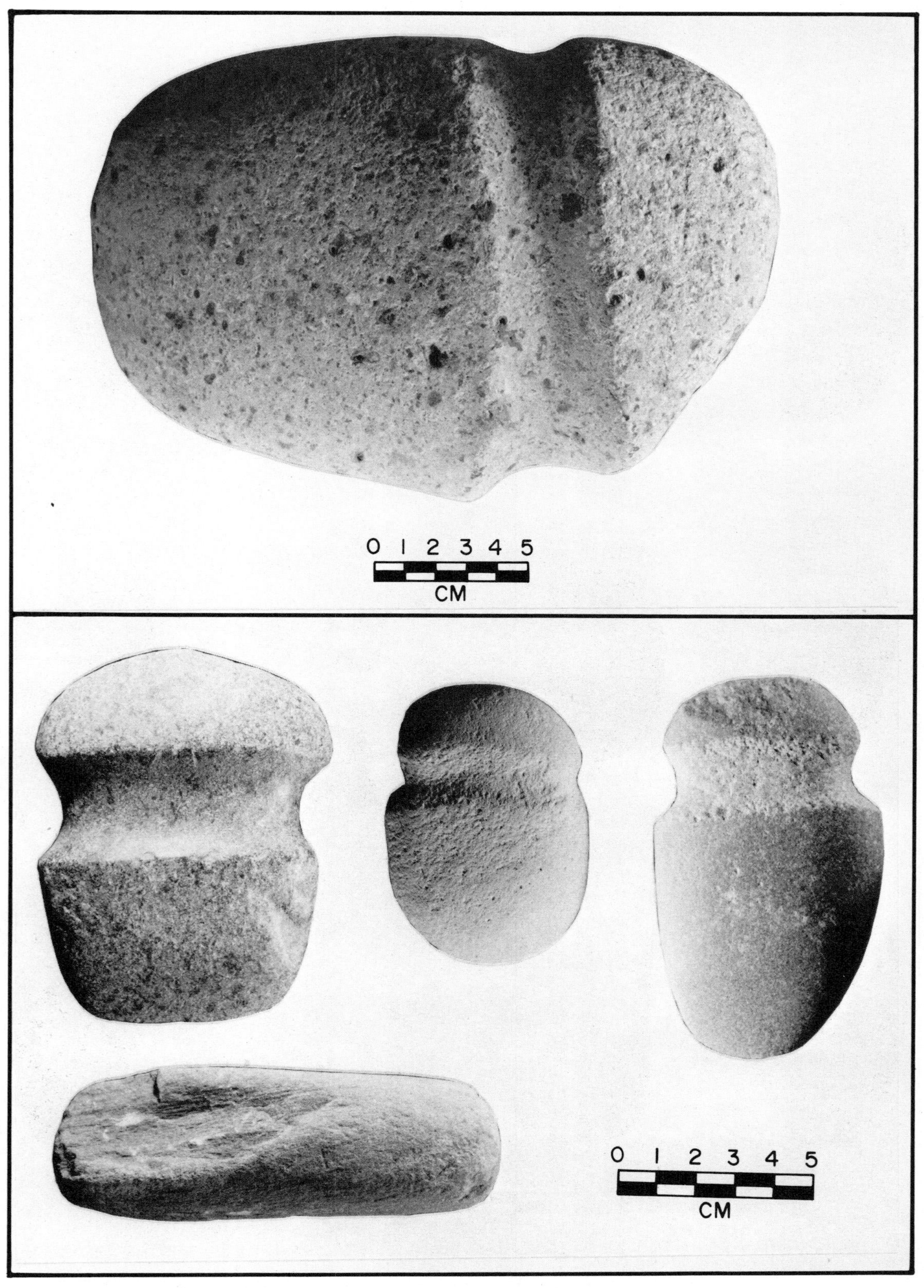

Figure A.30. Axes and tubular hammerstone or mano, Bullseye site. **Top** = large three-quarter grooved axe. **Bottom** = three-quarter grooved axes and mano.

Figure A.31. Full-grooved axes, Bullseye site.

REFERENCES CITED

Asch, Nancy, and David Asch
1982   *Early Vegetation of the Lower Illinois Valley Bottomlands*. Archeobotanical Laboratory No. 45. Ms. on file, Center for American Archeology, Kampsville, Illinois.

Batura, James, and David Leigh
1983   *Phase II Archeological Investigations at the Fox Pup and Gravity Sites, Nutwood Levee and Drainage District, Jersey and Greene Counties, Illinois*. St. Louis District Cultural Resource Management Report No. 6. Army Corps of Engineers, St. Louis.

Braun, David P., James B. Griffin, and Paul F. Titterington
1982   *The Snyders Mounds and Five Other Mound Groups in Calhoun County, Illinois*. Technical Report 13, Museum of Anthropology, University of Michigan, Ann Arbor.

Brown, James A., and Robert Vierra
1983   What happened in the Middle Archaic? Introduction to an Ecological Approach to Koster Site Archeology. In *Archaic Hunters and Gatherers of the American Midwest*, edited by J. Phillips, and J. Brown, pp. 165-195, Academic Press, New York.

Buikstra, Jane E.
1981   Mortuary Practices, Paleodemography, Paleopathology: A Case Study from the Koster Site (Illinois). In *The Archaeology of Death*, edited by Robert Chapman, Ian Kinnes, and Klavs Randaborg, pp. 123-132, Cambridge University Press, Cambridge, England.

Butzer, Karl
1977   *Geomorphology of the Lower Illinois Valley as a Spatial-Temporal Context for the Koster Archaic Site*. Reports of Investigation 34, Illinois State Museum, Springfield.

Charles, Douglas, and Jane E. Buikstra
1983   Archaic Mortuary Sites in the Central Mississippi Drainage: Distribution, Structure and Behavioral Implications. In *Archaic Hunters and Gatherers in the American Midwest*, edited by J. Phillips, and J. Brown, pp. 117-146. Academic Press, New York.

Charles, Douglas K., Stephen R. Leigh, and Jane E. Buikstra (editors)
n.d. *The Archaic and Woodland Cemeteries at the Elizabeth Site in the Lower Illinois Valley*. Center for American Archeology, Kampsville Archeological Center, Research Series 7, in press.

Conrad, Lawrence A.
1981   *An Introduction to the Archaeology of Upland West Central Illinois: A Preliminary Archaeological Survey of the Canton to Quincy Corridor for the Proposed FAP-407 Highway Project*. Archaeological Research Laboratory Report of Investigation No. 2, Western Illinois University, Macomb.

Cook, Thomas Genn
1976   *Koster: An Artifact Analysis of Two Archaic Phases in West-Central Illinois*. Prehistoric Records 1., Northwestern University Archeological Program, Evanston, Illinois.

Downey, C. E., D. R. Grantham, and J. B. Fehrenbacher
1974   *Soil Survey of Greene County.*   Illinois Agricultural Experiment Station Soil Report No.
93., U.S.D.A., U.S. Government Printing Office, Washington, D.C.

Farnsworth, Kenneth B., and David L. Asch
1986   Early Woodland Chronology, Artifact Styles, and Settlement Distribution in the Lower
Illinois Valley Drainage.   In *Early Woodland Archeology*, edited by K. B. Farnsworth, and T.
E. Emerson, pp. 326-448, Kampsville Seminars in Archeology 2.   Kampsville Archeological
Center, Kampsville, Illinois.

Farnsworth, Kenneth B., and John A. Walthall
1983   In the Path of Progress: Development of Illinois Highway Archeology and the FAP 408
Project.   *American Archeology* 3 (3):169-181.

Griffin, James B.
1955   Observations on the Grooved Axe in North America. *Pennsylvania Archeologist*
25(1):31-43.

1968   Observations on Illinois Prehistory in Late Pleistocene and Early Recent Times,   In
The Quaternary of Illinois, edited by R. E. Bergstrom, pp. 123-137, Special Publication 14,
College of Agriculture, University of Illinois, Urbana.

Hajic, Edwin R.
1981a *Shallow Subsurface Geology, Geomorphology and Limited Cultural Resource Investigations of the Nutwood Levee and Drainage District, Jersey and Greene Counties, Illinois.*
Reports of Investigations No. 108.   Contract Archeology Program, Center for American
Archeology.   Submitted to the Army Corps of Engineers, St. Louis District.

1981b *Shallow Subsurface Geology, Geomorphology and Limited Cultural Resource Investi-
gations of the Hartwell Levee and Drainage District, Greene County, Illinois.*   Reports of
Investigations No. 109.   Contract Archeology Program, Center for American Archeology.
Submitted to the Army Corps of Engineers, St. Louis District.

1983   *Shallow Subsurface Geology, Geomorphology and Limited Cultural Resource Inves-
tigations of the Hillview Levee and Drainage District, Scott and Greene Counties, Illinois.*   St.
Louis District Cultural Resource Management Report Number 5., Army Corps of Engineers,
St. Louis.

Hajic, Edwin R., and Harold Hassen
1980   *Geomorphological, Subsurface and Limited Cultural Resource Investigations of the Eldred
and Spankey Drainage and Levee Districts Project Area, Greene County, Illinois.* Reports of
Investigations 90.   Contract Archeology Program, Center for American Archeology.
Submitted to Army Corps of Engineers, St. Louis.

Hajic, Edwin R., and David S. Leigh
1985   *Shallow Subsurface Geology, Geomorphology and Limited Cultural Resource Investigations of the Meredosia Village and Meredosia Lake Levee and Drainage Districts, Scott,
Morgan and Cass Counties, Illinois.*   St Louis District Cultural Resource Management
Report Number 17.   Army Corps of Engineers, St. Louis.

Hassen, Harold (editor)
   1985a   *Middle Archaic Investigations Along the Illinois River Floodplain: Archeological Site Evaluations at the Quasar Site (11-Ge-136) and Bullseye (11-Ge-127) Sites Greene County, Illinois*. St. Louis District Cultural Resource Management Report Number 18. Army Corps of Engineers, St. Louis.

   1985b   *An Archeological Survey Along the Eastern Floodplain of the Lower Illinois River: Cultural Resource Survey of Selected Portions of the Meredosia and Meredosia Lake Drainage and Levee Districts, Scott, Cass and Morgan Counties, Illinois*. St. Louis District Cultural Resource Management Report Number 19. Army Corps of Engineers, St. Louis.

Hassen, Harold, and James M. Batura
   1983   *Archeological Investigations Along the Lower Illinois River Floodplain: Cultural Resource Surveys of the Hartwell and Nutwood Levee and Drainage Districts, Jersey and Greene Counties, Illinois*. St Louis District Cultural Resource Management Report Number 4. Army Corps of Engineers, St Louis.

Hassen, Harold, and Edwin R. Hajic
   1984   *Shallowly Buried Archeological Deposits and Geological Context: Archeological Survey in the Eldred and Spankey Drainage and Levee District, Greene County, Illinois*. St. Louis District Cultural Resource Management Report Number 8. Army Corps of Engineers, St. Louis.

Knoblock, Byron W.
   1939   *Bannerstones of the North American Indian*. Privately published. LaGrange, Illinois.

Kwas, Mary L.
   1981   Bannerstones as Chronological Markers in the Southeastern United States. *Tennessee Anthropologist* 6(2):144-171.

   1982   Bannerstones: An Historical Overview. *Journal of Alabama Archeology* 28(2):155-178.

Lurie, Rochelle
   1982   *Economic Models of Stone Tool Manufacture and Use: The Koster Site Middle Archaic*. Unpublished Ph.D. dissertation, Department of Anthropology, Northwestern University, Evanston, Illinois.

Perino, Gregory
   1961   Tentative Classification of Plummets in the Lower Illinois River Valley. *Central States Archeological Journal* 8(2):43-56.

Titterington, Paul
   1947   A Tube Pipe Filter. *Journal of the Illinois State Archaeological Society* 4(3):20-22.

   1950   Some Non-Pottery Sites in St. Louis Area. *Journal of the Illinois State Archaeological Society* 1:19-31.